DIARMUID GRIFFIN

SENTENCING SERIOUS SEX OFFENDERS

How Judges Decide when Discretion Is Wide

First published in Great Britain in 2025 by

Policy Press, an imprint of
Bristol University Press
University of Bristol
1–9 Old Park Hill
Bristol
BS2 8BB
UK
t: +44 (0)117 374 6645
e: bup-info@bristol.ac.uk

Details of international sales and distribution partners are available at
policy.bristoluniversitypress.co.uk

British Library Cataloguing in Publication Data
A catalogue record for this book is available from the British Library

ISBN 978-1-5292-3473-2 hardcover
ISBN 978-1-5292-3474-9 ePub
ISBN 978-1-5292-3475-6 ePdf

Cover design: Bristol University Press
Front cover image: Sasko Lazarov/RollingNews.ie
Bristol University Press and Policy Press use environmentally responsible print partners.
Printed and bound in Great Britain by CPI Group (UK) Ltd, Croydon, CR0 4YY

FSC
www.fsc.org
MIX
Paper | Supporting responsible forestry
FSC® C013604

Contents

List of tables

Acknowledgements

This book was difficult to research and write. While I am proud of the end product, the process in getting there was challenging. It would not have been possible without the support of some key people in my professional and personal life. Before thanking them, I would like to acknowledge the contributions of the 230 victims and survivors who sought justice through the criminal process. These cases form the foundation of this book and have significantly contributed to the development of sentencing principle and practice in Ireland.

Anthony O'Shea worked as a research assistant on this project. Not only was he excellent in the performance of this role, he was a pleasure to work alongside. His role was generously supported by the University of Galway's Post-Covid Research Support Fund. I would like to thank Rebecca Tomlinson and Grace Carroll at Policy Press/Bristol University Press for their guidance and help at all stages of the writing and production process.

David Doyle and Sinéad Ring offered valuable insights and comments on the book and were a great source of advice and encouragement. Mr Justice John Edwards provided important information on sentencing developments. I was lucky to have the support of friends and family and I would particularly like to thank Laurent Pech, Carmel Flynn, Tony Swaine, Hoffy Hosford, Liam Thornton, Aisling Doherty, Derek O'Brien, Deirdre Healy, Mike Caniffe, Louise Kennefick, Nicola Murphy as well as Fionn, Sinead, Rían and Caoila Griffin.

David Corcoran, Richard Kelly and Eoin Stapleton provided much needed input on book cover options, gave way too many pep talks to count and cooked lots of dinners to keep me going. Thanks lads!

And finally, I would like to acknowledge and thank my parents, Maurice and Lorraine, for their love and encouragement throughout the writing of this book, as well as in all the endeavours of life.

ONE

The apex of seriousness

Introduction

How and why judges decide to impose a particular sentence in an individual case has become a topic of intense public interest. It can be difficult to understand why sentences for those convicted of the same offence can vary so much. In cases of rape, for example, there have been instances where a person has received a life sentence while another person, convicted of the same offence, received a suspended sentence. While these types of cases may be very rare, such wide variety in outcome can sometimes generate public comment and controversy. When this happens, allegations of inconsistency in sentencing are often levied at the sentencing judge, as well as the system as a whole. Sentencing is one of the most publicly visible aspects of the criminal justice system. As a result, sentencing decisions can create a space for public debate, scrutiny and reflection on the purposes of punishment and the efficacy of the sentencing system.[1] The discourse on sentencing tends to revolve around an individual decision that is perceived to be unduly lenient in a case that, for whatever reason, captures the public imagination. The facts of the case and the outcome are debated across social, print and broadcast media and, after some time, public interest tends to wane as new stories emerge.

This book provides an opportunity to broaden and deepen the discourse on sentencing. To do so, it focuses on sentencing decisions in sexual offence cases at the apex of seriousness, using sentence length as the barometer of seriousness. This involves examining sentence outcomes resulting in 15 years' imprisonment up to (and including) life imprisonment in sexual offence cases decided over more than three decades in Ireland (from 1985 to 2022: n=108). Cases resulting in a sentence of this length are exceptional in two key respects. First, sexual offence cases that manage to reach a sentencing court are rare. A recent Central Statistics Office survey found nine in ten persons who experienced sexual violence as an adult did not disclose to *An Garda Síochána* (the Irish police).[2] There are similarly high rates of non-disclosure among adults who experienced sexual violence as a child (eight in ten). In the rare instances where a person does choose to disclose to the *Gardaí*, the likelihood of the case passing through the various stages of the criminal justice system and resulting in a conviction is low.[3] From 2017 to 2021, only one in five incidents of sexual violence reported to the *Gardaí* led to a charge or summons.[4] This is sometimes referred to as the 'justice gap' in sexual offence cases.[5]

The second reason that these cases may be viewed as exceptional is that even where a conviction has been secured, an outcome of 15 years to life imprisonment is extremely rare, and intentionally so. The courts have emphasised that a sentence of this length would only be appropriate in 'truly egregious' cases.[6] Looking at the available data over a 16-year period (2007 to 2023), 10.5 per cent of the total committals to prison for sexual offences were for persons sentenced to 10 years or more (including life imprisonment).[7] In 2021, Ireland reported just seven prisoners in custody serving a sentence of 20 years or more across all offences (excluding life imprisonment).[8] The rarity of these sentence outcomes provides an opportunity to explore how and why judges arrive at the conclusion that the offending is 'truly egregious' and warrants a penalty of 15 years to life imprisonment.

The analysis of sentencing decisions in serious sexual offence cases serves multiple purposes. First, it sheds light on judicial perceptions of what constitutes the most serious and aggravated version of these offences. Sentencing has a broader cultural significance and these assessments of seriousness can reflect and signal ideas about the hierarchy of harms in sexual offending. Information on sentencing in Ireland is very limited and this book takes steps to address this data deficit in an area of importance to many in Irish society and beyond. Second, through an examination of this specific category of offences, the book provides an opportunity to gain an understanding of how sentencing operates and the framework within which sentencing judges decide. It generates information relating to sentencing patterns and this can contribute to more fruitful and evidence-based discussions on the consistencies and/or disparities in sentencing choices. Third, Ireland is in a position where the discretion of judges may be placed under constraint in the future, through the adoption of sentencing guidelines. The research brings into focus the current state of play in terms of the use of the top end of the penalty range for sexual offences. This can inform policy debates as to what the future of sentencing in Ireland could or should look like.

Finally, this research provides insight into the role of a variety of factors, actors and structures in shaping sentencing decisions. The scrutiny of multi-level influences can contribute to the growing understanding of the interplay between criminal justice decision-makers and the role of local determinants and nuances.[9] The book deliberately widens the lens beyond traditional sentencing factors in order to highlight the complex array of influences operating within the sentencing ecosystem that have an impact on decision-making. As much of the research on sentencing focuses on a few select countries (often the US and UK), there is value in shifting the criminological gaze to a country with an under-explored sentencing system that has not experienced the erosion of discretion evident in other jurisdictions.[10] Thus, the analysis can provide fresh and diverse perspectives on sentencing patterns, policy, practice and reform. This introductory chapter details some of the key findings and insights that are further developed throughout the chapters of this book.

The discretion discourse

Comparatively speaking, the Irish sentencing system is known for affording judges wide discretion when deliberating on what sentence to impose.[11] This effectively means that judges have a lot of latitude when it comes to making sentencing choices. Discretion is often criticised as being one of the root causes of inconsistencies in sentencing decision-making. The logic goes that because judges have so much discretion, decisions are more a reflection of the individual judge than compliance with rules and guidelines. Where sentencing operates without sufficient structure the outcomes can be 'individually directed and un-patterned'.[12] Critics of discretion take the view that the individual freedom given to judges and the lack of structure or rules can result in inconsistent, unfair and arbitrary decision-making. Naturally, this is undesirable in a legal decision-making process. Such was the volume of criticism in relation to inconsistency that many countries adopted wide-ranging reforms designed to constrain discretion. These reforms tended to manifest in sentencing commissions that created guidelines for judges to comply with when sentencing.[13] Proponents of limiting or structuring discretion argue that these reforms will result in more rational, transparent and predictable sentencing outcomes.[14] The impact of these reforms on the discretion of judges varied, with rules and guidelines ranging from the rigid to the flexible.

There are also discretion devotees in the sentencing world. Many experts view discretion as a positive attribute of the sentencing process, arguing that it is best to trust the 'practical wisdom' of decision-makers who can draw on their professional experience and legal reasoning to arrive at an outcome that is proportionate, just and fair.[15] According to the proponents of discretion, this approach is a more effective and reliable method of decision-making than the rigid, systematised and artificial nature of a decision-making process governed by strict guidelines and regulations. The reality is that discretion requires rules and rules require discretion. As Tata points out, discretion can only exist because it is permitted by law.[16] Equally, rules and guidelines inevitably have an in-built level of discretion. Even in rigid structures, some level of discretion will often exist as the rules are interpreted and applied to the facts of the case by human actors – judges.

In Ireland, even though discretion is wide, judges must always operate within the legal rules. In order to arrive at a sentencing outcome, judges are tasked with synthesising all of the evidence presented at the sentencing hearing. They are required to arrive at an outcome that complies with the principles of sentencing as well as incorporating the purposes of punishment (such as rehabilitation or retribution). The sentence must reflect the seriousness of the offence, the culpability of the offender and the harm to the victim. A sentence may be increased as a result of aggravating factors that arise in the case (for example, the use of a weapon or abusing a position of trust). Similarly, a judge must also assess the mitigating factors present in the case (for example, a guilty plea or remorse) and apply an appropriate reduction to the sentence to reflect those mitigating circumstances.

When sentencing cases capture the public's attention through the media (and sexual offence cases often do), it is the seriousness of the offence and the harm to the victim that tends to be the focus, with less attention paid to the influence of mitigating factors on the sentence outcome. Depending on the level and extent of mitigation, the reduction in sentence may range from substantial to minimal, or even none at all. When there are very different outcomes in factually similar cases, the role that mitigation played in each case is an important factor to consider. The *outcome* may appear inconsistent when looking at the numerical sentence but the judge's *approach* in arriving at that sentence may well be consistent with the rules and practice of sentencing.

While other countries were engaging in wide-ranging reviews and reforms to address the perceptions and realities of inconsistency in sentencing, Ireland was paddling its own canoe. Occasional public and media discourse on disparities in decision-making was evident but this did not appear to cut through to the institutions with the ability to pursue reform. There has been little by way of legislative intervention to restrain sentencing practices. The principles of sentencing have mostly been developed by judges themselves, largely through judgments of the Court of Criminal Appeal, Court of Appeal and Supreme Court. These principles are usually general in nature and their purpose is to structure and shape the decision-making process of judges while still affording them a considerable degree of latitude.

A major shift happened in 2014 when the appellate courts issued judgments establishing sentencing bands to guide judges in calculating the seriousness of specific offences. Five years later, legislation established the Sentencing Guidelines and Information Committee and this body is tasked with creating guidelines for judges on sentencing (no guideline has been produced as of November 2024). While change may be afoot, the discretion of judges, guided by principles developed by the appellate courts, remains the cornerstone of sentencing in Ireland. Chapter 2 provides a detailed explanation of how sentencing works in practice and the principles and rules that structure and influence sentencing decisions in sexual offence cases. In the meantime, the impact of the legal framework as well as an analysis of a multitude of factors and drivers influencing decision-making in serious sexual offence cases is explored. The methodology employed to generate these findings is detailed in Chapter 3.

A choice within limits

There are a limited number of sexual offences where a penalty of 15 years to life imprisonment is available to a sentencing judge. These offences include rape, rape under section 4, aggravated sexual assault and defilement of a child under the age of 15. There are no minimum punishments for these offences and therefore the penalty can include anything from a community sanction to life imprisonment. A penalty range that encapsulates such a broad spectrum of outcomes allows for the widest of choice, at least in theory. In practice, as outlined, judges must ensure that their decisions comply with the principles of sentencing. Additionally, a recent decision of the Supreme Court established sentencing guidance for the offence of rape and this judgment detailed the factors that might justify the imposition of a sentence of 15 years to life imprisonment.[17]

In terms of the selection of sentences in this study, judges primarily chose to impose sentences at the lower and higher end of the range. The most frequently selected sentences were 15 years' imprisonment (two in five cases) or life imprisonment (one in five cases). The remainder of sentences imposed were greater than 15 years but rarely exceeded 20 years' imprisonment. Without a numerical limit, a sentence of 30 or 40 years could conceivably be imposed in a serious case and, in some countries, sentences of this length are permitted.[18] In Ireland, it is clear that the practice is to limit determinate sentences to a maximum of 20 years, except in very exceptional circumstances. Judges suspended a part of the custodial sentence in over half of determinate sentence cases (52 per cent) and this had the effect of reducing the reality of time served in custody. This part suspension was often contingent on the offender complying with conditions set by the judge. These conditions tended to focus on managing the risk of reoffending on release back into the community.

As the ultimate penalty available in the State, life imprisonment should only be imposed for the 'most serious crimes'.[19] What this means in practice was not always clear when comparing cases of life imprisonment with determinate sentences of 15 years or more in sexual offence cases. A factor of significance that emerged in some cases related to an assessment that the defendant posed a risk of reoffending on release and was viewed by the sentence judge as a 'danger to the public'.[20] Judges valued the fact that a consequence of imposing life imprisonment meant that release back into the community would be determined through the parole process. Ordinarily, a life sentence prisoner will only be released when parole decision-makers are of the view that the risk of reoffending has been reduced to an acceptable level.[21] The selection of determinate and life sentences is discussed in Chapter 3 and this includes a deconstruction of the component parts of these sentences to better understand their meaning. For now, it is useful to set out some of the key factors that influenced sentencing outcomes of this severity.

The multiplicity of offending

The most significant factor that emerged in analysing these cases related to the volume of offending being dealt with at each sentencing hearing. Judges were not simply sentencing for a single offence. In almost all cases the defendant had committed multiple offences (94 per cent). The volume of offending in some instances was astounding, with a number of cases exceeding 100 offences. In addition, half of all cases involved multiple victims of sexual violence and almost two thirds involved multiple incidents (63 per cent). A total of 230 victims of sexual violence were identified across 108 cases. Cases where adults were victimised usually involved multiple offences committed during a single incident whereas in child sexual abuse cases the offending tended to be perpetrated over a prolonged period of time. For example, in one child sexual abuse case the sentencing judge was dealing with offences that were committed over a 23-year period.

Judges are required to impose an individual sentence for each offence being dealt with at the sentencing hearing. An important choice then arises – whether to order these individual sentences to run concurrently (all at the same time) or consecutively (one after the other). The analysis shows that judges imposed concurrent sentences in 86 per cent of multi-conviction cases. Imposing concurrent sentences in multi-crime cases has long been a part of sentencing practice and this is also reflected in the principles developed by the appellate courts. The consensus is that while the decision is within the discretion of the judge, consecutive sentences should be imposed sparingly. What this means is that the multi-crime offender will effectively receive a bulk discount due to the fact that these offences are all being dealt with at the same hearing and have been ordered to run concurrently.[22] To minimise the benefit of this, judges must take into consideration the totality of the offending when imposing a sentence in a multi-crime case and may adjust the sentence upwards accordingly. As a result, the sentence imposed in these cases should be viewed as a reflection of the volume of offending in the case as a whole rather than a single sentence for a single crime.

In cases such as these, judges find themselves in a challenging situation. On the one hand, they must have regard for the general policy and practice that emphasises a preference for concurrent sentences, as well as ensuring the sentence remains within the numerical limits of judicial practice (usually up to 20 years or life imprisonment). This means that it may be difficult to reflect the breadth, depth and seriousness of the offending that is present in these cases. On the other hand, deciding to impose consecutive sentences in cases where a multitude of serious offences have been committed would result in a sentence so long that it would far exceed the lifespan of the offender. These issues, as well as the impact of selecting a determinate or life sentence, are discussed in Chapter 3.

Sentencing crimes committed against adult victims

In assessing case-related factors influencing sentencing outcomes, it is useful to distinguish between cases where the victim(s) of sexual violence were adults (45 of 108) or children (63 of 108). In cases involving adult victims, a remarkably consistent and narrow fact pattern emerged. The perpetrators were all male and were often either strangers to the victim (65 per cent) or met the victim within 24 hours of the incident (18 per cent). All of the victims were female and most were victimised in early adulthood. These offences were frequently committed in a public place and referred to by judges as a 'random attack'. The cases also involved serious levels of violence, including the use of weapons or the threat of their use (58 per cent) and death threats (51 per cent). Although the attack was often random, there was evidence that the offending was planned and premeditated (16 per cent) and involved the tricking of the victim (29 per cent) rendering them more vulnerable to attack. Sentencing judges viewed all of these factors as increasing the culpability of the defendant. The level of harm caused to these victims was of critical importance to judges, referencing the physical and psychological impact of the offending and recognising the long-term effects of this type of victimisation. The assessment of harm caused was informed by victim impact statements which were identifiable in 62 per cent of cases.

At a broader level, factors more directly related to the defendant were of significance. Of most import was the previous criminal history of the offender, which was referenced by judges in two thirds of cases (67 per cent). Three out of five of those with a previous criminal history had been convicted of sexual offences. A previous criminal history contributed to an assessment that the offender posed a risk of reoffending, as did professional input from Probation Officers, psychologists and psychiatrists. Judges made reference to concerns in relation to the risk of reoffending in just over half of all cases (51 per cent). These offenders were described as a 'grave threat' to the public.[23] Of course, judges are required to consider a reduction to the sentence where there are mitigating factors. Aside from the entering of a guilty plea (56 per cent of cases), the level of mitigation was limited.

Given the specific fact pattern that emerged from the analysis, it is worthwhile considering whether broader cultural beliefs about rape are playing a role in judicial decision-making. There are some obvious parallels between these cases and what criminologists and feminists describe as the 'real rape' myth.[24] This refers to a misperception that rape often involves a violent attack by a stranger with a weapon at night-time in a public place, causing physical injury. The prevalence of 'stranger rapes' in these cases raises questions as to whether judges are reserving sentences of this severity based, in part, on the relationship between the parties and the perception that 'stranger rape' is more serious and/or harmful. Research on sexual violence indicates that the majority of rapes are perpetrated by assailants known to the victim and levels of violence or harm towards the victim cannot be presumed based on the nature of the relationship.[25] Further, international studies have demonstrated that there can be a reluctance among sentencing judges to impose an adequate sentence to reflect the gravity of the offence where, for example, the perpetrator is the partner or ex-partner of the victim.[26] It is certainly possible that the relationship between the parties may be operating as a shadow factor that is having an impact on sentence outcomes. Given the consistency in terms of fact patterns, it is worth reflecting on the potential impact of 'rape myths' on sentencing decision-makers and this is further explored, alongside a detailed discussion of sentencing factors influencing outcomes, in Chapter 4.

Sentencing crimes of child sexual abuse

In cases where children were victims (63), judges were tasked with addressing the breadth, depth and depravity of offending at the sentencing hearing. While there were 63 defendants, there was a total of 159 victims of sexual violence across all cases. The offending in these cases commenced when the child or children were of a young age. In over two thirds of cases, victimisation began when the child or children were aged 10 or younger. There was more diversity in terms of the gender of victims of child sexual abuse, with two thirds of the victims being female and a third being male.

Multiple sexual offences were committed in all cases. In some cases, the volume of offences committed was staggering, with one in six cases involving 50 offences or more. The impact of a decision to impose concurrent or consecutive sentences was at its most consequential in these cases, as consecutive sentences would almost certainly result in a sentence that far exceeded the life of the offender. At the same time, a decision to impose concurrent sentences meant that it was difficult to reflect the breadth of the offending within the existing limitations, particularly where there were multiple victims.

In addition to the multiplicity of offending, a highly significant aggravating factor in these cases was that the perpetrator abused a position of trust or misused a dominant position within a family. The perpetrator was either a father or step-father to the victim in 45 per cent of instances. Outside of this, in almost all cases there was some form of relationship with the child (or the family members of the child) and the perpetrator breached that trust in the relationship. Judges took into consideration the harm caused to the victim(s) noting in particular the serious and long-term consequences resulting from victimisation in childhood. A victim impact statement was identified in 78 per cent of cases. Aggravating factors relating to the level and extent of violence perpetrated against the victim(s) were identified by judges including, for example: special violence; additional and gratuitous sexual perversions; the use of death threats; and the use of implements of violence. Similar to cases involving adult victims, a guilty plea was the most prevalent mitigating factor (70 per cent of cases). As the nature and extent of offending was so severe in these cases the impact of mitigation on sentence reduction was often modest.

A previous criminal history was less prevalent than in cases involving adult victims (32 per cent of cases). However, given the volume of offending, the number of victims and the prolonged and sustained nature of the abuse, it is more accurate to state that the offending did not come to the attention of the authorities at the time it was committed and, as a consequence, it was all being dealt with at the same sentencing hearing. Victim(s) often only disclosed the offending to the *Gardaí* as an adult, with a delay of over five years identifiable from the commission of the last offence to accessing the justice system in 38 per cent of cases.

Legal, societal and structural barriers to disclosing child sexual abuse created a culture of silence in Ireland for much of the twentieth century and this had an impact on the likelihood of these cases reaching a sentencing court. In terms of legal barriers, up until the 1990s the courts adopted a stringent approach to permitting cases of delay to proceed based on the defendant's right to a fair trial.[27] A growth in public awareness of child sexual abuse in Ireland as well as a 'torrent' of non-recent child sexual abuse cases coming before the courts during this time widened the scope for the prosecution of these cases.[28] There was an increase in cases of child sexual abuse in this study from the late 1990s onwards. This demonstrates the importance in mapping and analysing broader social and legal evolutions when assessing cases that come before the courts and how they are dealt with, if and when they get there. For instance, the findings from a recent report on child sexual abuse in schools run by Catholic religious orders has brought about a commitment to establish a statutory commission of inquiry.[29] This may lead to a greater number of disclosures by non-recent victims to the *Gardaí* in the future. These issues and the factors arising in cases involving child sexual abuse are discussed in Chapter 5.

Factoring in judges

In order to gain further insight into how judges decide, it is worthwhile shifting the lens of analysis onto the individuals making these decisions and the environment within which they operate. It is useful to think about the role of judges as occupants of one layer of the sentencing ecosystem – a complex network of actors, relationships, structures and institutions that shape and influence sentencing outcomes, whether directly or obliquely.[30] Sentencing is often viewed as being within the exclusive domain of the individual judge but judges do not operate in a silo and their decisions should be interpreted as collaborative and reliant on the input of others. It is important to be cognisant of the fact that a judge is making a decision at the end stage of a process where prior decisions, assessments and submissions have been made by a number of agencies and actors. The cases that come before the courts for sentencing are contingent on the number and type of victims that choose to disclose (or not), the decisions by the police and prosecution as to which types of cases to progress (or not) and the decisions by juries to convict (or not) when presented with different facts in sexual offence cases. When a case does come before a court for sentencing there are a range of criminal justice professionals, witnesses and parties to the case that submit information and provide evidence to the judge. For example, a report from a Probation Officer prepared for the judge indicating the defendant's likelihood of reoffending or the submission of evidence detailing the harm caused to the victim may have a real impact on the final sentence outcome.

The sexual offences that are the focus of this study are almost exclusively dealt with by a small group of judges that sit at the Central Criminal Court. Sexual offences make up the majority of these judges sentencing workload (92 per cent of cases).[31] By virtue of regularly dealing with sexual offence cases, they are operating from a stronger knowledge base in their decision-making when compared with judges in other courts around the country who deal with a much more diverse caseload. Somewhat incredibly, one judge was responsible for 45 per cent of the sentencing decisions in this study. This judge was the only full-time member of the Central Criminal Court for an extended period. It is not at all surprising that there are high levels of consistency in these cases given that almost half of them were decided by the same judge. What is interesting is that this consistency extended to the decisions of many of the other 23 judges responsible for outcomes in this study. This indicates that factors, fact patterns and perceptions of seriousness are somewhat embedded among this cohort of judges.

A significant number of these sentences were appealed (43 per cent) and this provided a direct line of review and accountability to this small group of decision-makers. Almost all of the appeals challenged the severity of the sentence imposed and applicants were successful in securing a reduction in their sentence in 50 per cent of these appeals. The strong probability that a sentencing decision will be subsequently reviewed and scrutinised by colleagues is likely to shape the decision itself and how the judge articulates the reasons for their decision. This regular feedback loop may further embed patterns and factors in decision-making, with judges being aware of their sentencing decisions being upheld or reduced on appeal and the reasons for this. This sentencing echo chamber is specific to sexual offence cases appearing before the Central Criminal Court. It highlights the additional insights on sentencing that can be garnered from examining the individual and institutional environment within which these decisions are made.

Of course, outside of the impact on an individual case, appellate decisions have the potential to develop sentencing principles, the specific purpose of which is to structure and inform future decisions of the sentencing courts. These judgments are referred to as the 'sentencing canon' and they are designed to assist judges in the exercise of their 'principled discretion'.[32] There has been a noticeable uptick in the volume of judgments on sentencing being issued by the appellate courts over the last decade or so, such that even the most studious of judges might have difficulty keeping up with the breadth of principles scattered across an ever-expanding canon. There was an observable increase in the quality, clarity and structure of sentencing remarks in the latter part of the study and the focus of appellate judgments in setting out best practice to follow in sentencing is likely to have contributed to this. In 2019, the Supreme Court issued a judgment setting out sentencing bands and relevant factors for each band in cases of rape. This included a band for 15 years to life imprisonment. Although the guidance was issued towards the end of the study, many of the factors set out by the Supreme Court were evident in the case analysis. This is not surprising as the factors established in guidance judgments are based on previous decisions at trial and appellate level (see Chapter 2).

Judges are also permitted to exercise their 'practical wisdom' in deliberating on a sentencing outcome.[33] Practical wisdom is key to the discretionary model of decision-making and it permits judges to draw on their professional experience and subjective judgement in deliberating on sentencing outcomes.[34] Due to its unspecific nature, and being tied to the internal thought processes, musings and experiences of the judge, its influence on outcomes is difficult to analyse. A list of aggravating and mitigating factors is far easier to measure. Yet, there was evidence of 'practical wisdom' when examining the sentencing remarks of judges in these cases. It was common for judges to use their own professional experiences as a barometer in assessing and expressing the gravity of the offending. For example, one judge stated that the offending was 'the most grievous sexual assault I have ever come across in my career'.[35]

Judges also engaged in the use of emotive language to convey the level of seriousness, referring to the offending as 'unbelievable'[36] and 'unspeakable'[37] while describing the offender as 'evil'[38] and 'monstrous'.[39] In an effort to indicate and express the exceptional nature of the offending, there was evidence of a departure from the typical language of restraint associated with judicial reasoning. Sentencing remarks are an important record of the reasons for a judge's decision and are relied upon by judicial and legal colleagues, particularly when there is an appeal. But the language used must also be interpreted in the context of the need for the judge to communicate the sentencing message to a wider audience, such as victims, defendants, the media and the public. These communication choices may be a way of expressing to this audience that the judge viewed the offending as being at the apex of seriousness.

There are also macro-level influences that can inform and change sentencing policy and outcomes, such as legislative, media, social and political drivers. For example, in the 1990s a series of serious sexual offence cases caused comment and controversy due largely to the fact that judges were required to reduce the sentence based on the defendant entering a guilty plea. This was further stoked by the comments of a sentencing judge expressing frustration with the limitations placed upon judges dealing with this type of scenario. Public concern, driven by the media, resulted in politicians raising the need for reform, which led to legislation being passed that permitted judges to impose life imprisonment in exceptional cases, even when the defendant pleaded guilty. The analysis in this study shows that these reforms impacted decisions after the passing of this legislation. A more detailed discussion of these influences and their contributions to judicial decision-making is explored in Chapter 6.

Conclusion

This book engages with the complexity of sentencing through taking a broad and holistic look at the various drivers shaping the decision-making landscape in serious sexual offence cases. The data analysis indicates that there appears to be a consensus across decision-makers regarding the level of conduct, culpability and harm warranting a penalty in the top range. This consistency may be viewed by some as evidence of the benefits of the discretionary model of sentencing, but consistency needs to be interrogated and its meaning properly understood. One key concern is that the narrow pattern of facts resulting in sentences of this severity may entrench certain patterns and perceptions as being representative of the apex of sexual violence. This may have the effect of inadvertently excluding other acts of sexual violence of equal seriousness that do not fit this narrow pattern. Also, consistency in itself cannot be the sole goal of sentencing. A system that consistently produces outcomes that are unduly severe or lenient should not be viewed positively simply because those decisions are consistent. Ideally, sentences should also be moderate and proportionate. And on that note, the next chapter examines the principles of sentencing in Ireland and how they are specifically designed to produce proportionate outcomes.

TWO

Getting to guidance

Introduction

The principles developed by the appellate courts in Ireland are a critical starting point in understanding how judges decide. Although sentencing practice in Ireland is notable for its discretionary nature, judges must comply with the principles of sentencing. O'Malley notes that a 'sentencing canon' of appellate judgments has developed over the decades, the purpose of which is to facilitate sentencing judges in exercising their 'principled discretion'.[1] This chapter explores the key principles of sentencing as well as discussing a number of important developments that have had an impact on sentencing choices. The chapter starts in 1985 with a decision to impose a sentence of 21 years for the offence of rape.[2] At the time, counsel for the defence remarked that, to his knowledge, this was the most significant sentence imposed in the history of the State for an offence outside of murder. The case led to an important Supreme Court decision that effectively threw cold water on the idea of the appellate courts developing offence-specific guidance for sentencing judges to assist in their decision-making. The case had serious ramifications for sentencing over the following decades and this is why 1985 was chosen as the starting point for cases in this study (n=108 from 1985 to 2022).

While many countries were making various attempts to address the perception that discretion was a barrier to achieving consistency in sentencing, Ireland was doubling down on its dedication to discretion. The typical judicial response to the criticism that discretion was leading to inconsistent sentences was to rebuff this with the contention that constraining discretion would actually result in greater disparities and unfairness.[3] The argument goes that limiting discretion would mean that a sentencing judge would not be able to tailor the sentence to the individual before the court. Irrespective of the merits of this position, there has been a growing sentiment that sentencing is unpredictable, at least for those looking at it from the outside in. The situation for sentencing judges was also very challenging. There was little by way of guidance through legislation. Information on sentencing patterns and outcomes for different offences was completely lacking. In addition to this, the penalty range for offences is often very broad. A person convicted of the offence of rape could receive a community sanction, a suspended sentence, a short, medium or long determinate sentence or a sentence of life imprisonment.

There has been a notable shift away from judicial scepticism surrounding the structuring of discretion. A movement towards the development of guidance for specific offences started in the mid-2000s but really took off in 2014 when a 'quiet revolution' in sentencing occurred.[4] The Court of Criminal Appeal departed from the long-standing position that the appellate courts should refrain from providing trial judges with sentencing guidance for offences. The court issued a number of decisions that set out sentencing bands for specific offences, detailing the factors that might place the offending in the lower-to-higher range of the penalty for the offence. So, for example, where the maximum penalty for an offence is 15 years, the appellate court might specify the lower band as zero to five years, the medium band as 5 to 10 years and the higher band as over 10 years. The court, in its judgment, will then give examples of factors that might place the offending into each band. A major influencing factor in providing guidance was access to information on sentencing patterns for the offence under consideration. Although data generation on sentencing still remains in its infancy in Ireland, the analysis of previous sentencing decisions and appeals is central in formulating sentencing bands in guidance judgments. This chapter examines these developments as they relate to sexual offences, as well as setting out how sentencing works in practice. This lays the foundation for the analysis of serious sexual offence cases in subsequent chapters.

The *Tiernan* legacy

For almost 30 years there was relative stagnation in terms of judicially developed guidance on sentencing for specific offences. This set Ireland apart from many other common law countries that were taking steps either through the appellate courts, legislative reform or policy changes to limit or structure sentencing discretion. For example, in England and Wales, the Court of Appeal began to develop guidance judgments on sentencing from the 1970s onwards.[5] A legal reason for the lack of movement in Ireland on this issue can largely be attributed to the *Tiernan* case, a Supreme Court decision from the 1980s. The decision appeared to establish an insuperable barrier to the creation of judicially developed guidance by the appellate courts that could assist sentencing judges in their deliberations. A different interpretation of the implications of this decision was provided by the Court of Criminal Appeal in 2014, but the net effect of *Tiernan* in the intervening years was to put the idea that the appellate courts could develop offence-specific guidance to assist sentencing judges on pause.

At the sentencing hearing, Edward Tiernan and his co-defendant Robert Nolan were each sentenced to 21 years in prison. The judge described the offending as 'abominable and bestial' and 'the worst' case he had heard in his 45-year career in the legal profession.[6] Tiernan and Nolan, along with another man, forcibly entered the car of the victim and her boyfriend. The victim's boyfriend was then locked in the boot. The victim was dragged to a nearby field where she was subject to a gang-rape and this included 'acts of sexual perversion'.[7] Later that day, the perpetrators were interviewed by the *Gardaí*. They admitted their crimes and subsequently pleaded guilty to the charges against them.

The judge, in his sentencing remarks, noted that there were a number of aggravating factors that influenced the severity of the sentence imposed. It was a gang-rape and the victim was raped on more than one occasion. There was violence used against the victim in addition to the act of rape. The rape was performed by an act of abduction and her boyfriend was falsely imprisoned. Further, it was established that the offending resulted in the victim being diagnosed with a serious nervous disorder which lasted six months after the offending. She was unable to attend work during this period. Tiernan had a number of previous convictions, including for acts of violence and gross indecency. Nolan, who was 19 at the time of the offending, had no previous convictions and it was noted that he did not have sexual intercourse with the victim. His legal counsel argued that while he had aided and abetted the offending, he was under the influence of the older men, who were in their 20s. The judge imposed these sentences having weighed the aggravating and mitigating factors in the case.

The severity of this sentence was appealed by Tiernan and Nolan to the Court of Criminal Appeal. The barrister for Tiernan remarked that it was 'difficult to know what to say as the crime was so horrific' but argued that a sentence of 21 years was too severe.[8] The Court of Criminal Appeal decided to reduce Nolan's sentence to 12 years on account of his more limited role in the offending and his age. Tiernan's appeal was dismissed but was then appealed to the Supreme Court.[9]

In their judgment, the Supreme Court addressed the issue as to whether the court could or should produce guidance for sentencing judges for the offence of rape. In considering this, the court observed that there was a lack of statistics or information before the court establishing patterns of sentencing for the offence. In addition, noting the 'fundamental necessity' in maintaining judicial discretion in imposing an appropriate sentence, Chief Justice Finlay stated: 'I would doubt that it is appropriate for an appellate court to appear to be laying down any standardisation or tariff of penalty for cases.'[10] For these reasons, no guidance was provided. Tiernan's sentence was ultimately reduced to 17 years on account of the early admission of offending and the entering of a guilty plea. The Supreme Court decided that the sentencing judge did not give enough weight to these mitigating factors. Whether intentionally or otherwise, the consequence of this decision was that guidance for sentencing judges was not properly considered again until a departure from this position in 2014. This meant that judges were reliant on the general principles of sentencing when determining what sentence to impose. It is important to take a look at how those sentencing principles operate in practice before exploring the shift towards guidance in 2014.

The sentencing hearing

Judges must operate within the penalty range for the offence as well as adhering to any principles established by the courts and legislative requirements. In order to determine the appropriate sentence within the penalty range, a sentencing hearing is held after the defendant has been convicted of the offence. It is the sole responsibility of the judge to determine the sentence. In order to do so, the judge should be fully and accurately informed in relation to the offence and the offender.[11] Evidence will be presented in court by both the prosecution and defence in this regard. The sentencing hearing must also comply with the constitutional right to fair procedures that govern the trial process.[12]

The Director of Public Prosecutions (the DPP) plays an important role in informing the judge of the facts of the case as well as the level of involvement of the defendant. Evidence from *An Garda Síochána* or other witnesses will be presented to assist in this regard and this evidence can be challenged by the defence.[13] This information is of particular importance in a case where a defendant has pleaded guilty as there has not been a trial establishing the facts of the case. The practice of providing a sentencing court with a pre-sentence report from the Probation Service began in 1999, with risk assessments being consistently incorporated in these reports from 2005 onwards.[14] Reports and evidence may be presented by other professionals or non-professionals at the hearing. A victim impact statement may be submitted to the court if the victim so chooses.[15] Defendants may exercise their right to present evidence and make submissions to the court in the hopes of securing a lenient sentence.[16] There is 'considerable latitude' for defendants to make submissions in support of sentence mitigation and the rules of evidence are not as strict as they would be in a trial context.[17] Having heard all the evidence at the sentencing hearing, judges must then apply the relevant law to arrive at a proportionate sentence.

The principle of proportionality

Judges are tasked with determining the appropriate punishment for 'differing manifestations of the same offence'.[18] In Ireland, this is achieved through the application of the principle of proportionality. This principle is the focal point of sentencing practice and it was developed by the appellate courts to guide sentencing judges in their decisions. The principle is distributive in nature and requires that the sentence imposed must be proportionate to the gravity of the offence and the personal circumstances of the offender. Although the principle is long established, the appellate courts have continued to develop and elaborate on its meaning over time.

So how does proportionality work in practice? The Supreme Court, in the 1990s, stated that sentencing judges should adopt a staged or two-tiered approach.[19] First, the judge should examine where the offending falls within 'the range of penalties applicable to the offence'.[20] The completion of this step should result in what is called the headline sentence. The headline sentence may be expressed as a specific number or as a sentence range. An evaluation of the gravity of the offence will include an assessment of the harm caused, the culpability of the offender, as well as incorporating any aggravating factors in the case. An aggravating factor will result in a more severe penalty than would ordinarily be the case for a typical offence of this nature. These factors can be general in nature (for example, the premeditated nature of the offence) or they can be related to a specific offence (for example, abusing a position of trust in the case of a sexual offence). Aggravating (and mitigating) factors are derived from the 'sentencing canon' of judgments developed by the appellate courts over decades.[21] Where the defendant is being sentenced for multiple offences, an individual sentence should be imposed for each offence and then the judge will decide whether to order these sentences to run concurrently (all at the same time) or consecutively (one after the other) (see Chapter 3).

Having selected the penalty to be imposed based on the seriousness of the offence, the second step requires the court to assess the personal circumstances of the offender and any mitigating factors arising. Mitigating factors can include: offence-related mitigation (for example, partial excuse for the behaviour); response to charges (for example, guilty plea, remorse, cooperation with investigation); and personal mitigation (for example, absence of previous convictions, disability, age). An appropriate reduction should then be applied to the headline sentence. Following this process should, in theory at least, result in a judge arriving at a sentence that is fair and proportionate.

Prior to the Supreme Court decision in the 1990s, a sentencing outcome was almost always arrived at through 'pure instinctive synthesis'.[22] This is where a judge takes into consideration all factors relevant to the case together and arrives at a sentencing outcome. The two-step approach favoured by the Supreme Court encouraged judges to separate out, numerically speaking, step one (the gravity of the offence) from step two (the circumstances of the offender). While the two-tiered system is considered best practice and important in ensuring consistency of approach in sentencing, the appellate courts have accepted that judges are still permitted to employ pure instinctive synthesis.[23]

Judges are not required to provide a weight for each individual factor that cumulatively contributed to the headline sentence or the mitigation applied to the headline sentence. There is often no specific numerical weight provided for individual factors (such as the guilty plea or use of a weapon) in cases where there are many factors in aggravation or mitigation. Judges continue to employ the 'instinctive synthesis' approach in arriving at an outcome for each individual step. The appellate courts have made it clear that sentencing in Ireland is not amenable to mathematical calculation. The Court of Appeal recently stated that 'the sentencing judge will bring to bear his or her professional experience, intuition and subjective judgment and arrive at a [sentence]'.[24] This 'practical wisdom' is shaped through the 'sentencing canon' of appellate decisions that facilitate judges in exercising their 'principled discretion'.[25] Basically, what this means is that while judges are to be guided by the principles of the appellate courts, they still retain considerable flexibility and discretion in their application. At the same time, a failure to properly apply these principles may lead to an appeal against sentence and the appellate court may determine that there has been an error of principle. The sentence may be reduced, increased or varied as a result.

Finally, judges should also consider the purposes of punishment when deliberating on an appropriate sentence. The appellate courts have acknowledged that sentencing will involve balancing the penal objectives of retribution, rehabilitation, incapacitation and deterrence.[26] Perhaps the most frequently referenced purpose of punishment in sentencing practice is rehabilitation. Incorporating a rehabilitative component is viewed by the appellate courts as important in sentencing and a failure to do so has resulted in a reduction in sentence on appeal.[27] It appears to enjoy some level of priority over deterrence or incapacitation.[28] Judges should provide the opportunity for rehabilitation in every case 'no matter how bad'[29] in order to leave 'light at the end of the tunnel'.[30] In doing so, a judge should assess the credibility of evidence that rehabilitative work has already been undertaken or that there is a realistic rehabilitative programme in place for the future.[31]

It is not always easy to reconcile some of the purposes of punishment with the principle of proportionality when deliberating on a sentence. For example, a sentence imposed with the purpose of incapacitating an offender that poses a risk to the community does not fit easily with a principle focused primarily on the offence(s) committed in the past and the circumstances of the person. It is fair to say that the relationship between the principle of proportionality and the purposes of punishment has not yet been fully worked out when looking at cases in the 'sentencing canon'. Some of the legal and practical difficulties arising from the risk of reoffending being considered as a factor in imposing life imprisonment is dealt with in Chapter 3.

Sentencing remarks

Having heard the evidence and applied the principle of proportionality to arrive at a sentencing outcome, the judge will then deliver their sentencing remarks in court. These remarks communicate the sentence imposed and the reasons for it. While it might be assumed that a judge should always give reasons for their decision, this only became a requirement relatively recently. In 2004, the Court of Criminal Appeal noted that there did not appear to be an obligation on sentencing judges to give reasons but that it was desirable that they do so.[32] In practice, some form of reasoning has almost always been provided by judges although it is fair to say the quality of sentencing remarks has increased in the last 15 years. Since 2008, sentencing judges have a duty to explicitly go through the process in arriving at the sentencing outcome.[33] A failure to provide sufficient detail on these 'thought processes' may result in the appellate courts deciding that there was an error of principle in sentencing with the likelihood being that a new sentence would be imposed.[34]

As already noted, judges are not required to express the numerical weight applied to each individual factor taken into consideration when delivering their sentencing remarks.[35] The difficulty with this is that it can be unclear how much weight has actually been placed on, for example, a guilty plea in mitigating the sentence. There is no specific policy on the numerical weight to be applied as a result of a guilty plea although it is generally accepted that the discount should range from between 15 to 30 per cent of the headline sentence.[36] The judge might indicate that total mitigation required a reduction of three years. But if there are multiple mitigating factors, as is often the case, it is not possible to identify the weight applied to the guilty plea specifically. If the sentence is appealed, the appellate courts may be left somewhat in the dark as to the weight attributed to each factor. This makes it challenging to establish whether the sentencing judge has made an error in the case. In such circumstances, the appellate courts may have to engage in some level of educated guess work in an attempt to reverse engineer a sentence that may be 'inadequately reasoned'.[37] Having considered the principles and practice of sentencing generally, it is important to now examine the legal framework for sexual offences and the penalty range applicable to these offences.

Sentencing serious sexual offences

There are a limited number of offences where the penalty range includes a potential outcome of 15 years to life imprisonment.

The offences of rape,[38] rape under s.4,[39] aggravated sexual assault,[40] and defilement of a child under the age of 15[41] all have a maximum sentence of life imprisonment.[42] The maximum sentence for the offence of incest by a male has varied over the years but since the 1990s the maximum penalty has been life imprisonment.[43] In 2017, a newly formulated offence of a sexual act with a protected person was passed by legislation and this included a penalty where a maximum term of life imprisonment may be imposed.[44] In this research, it was only possible to source sentence outcomes of 15 years or more for rape, rape under s.4, aggravated sexual assault and defilement of a child under the age of 15.

The offence of rape is narrow and gender-specific in nature – 'a man commits rape if he has unlawful sexual intercourse with a woman who at the time of the intercourse does not consent to it, and at that time he knows that she does not consent to the intercourse or he is reckless as to whether she does or does not'.[45] In 1990, given this narrow definition, the legislature created two new offences – rape under s.4 and aggravated sexual assault. Rape under s.4 criminalises a sexual assault that involves the penetration of the vagina by an object as well as penetration of the anus or mouth by a penis. Aggravated sexual assault criminalises a sexual assault that involves 'serious violence or the threat of serious violence or is such as to cause injury, humiliation or degradation of a grave nature to the person assaulted'.[46] Prior to these reforms, much of this non-consensual sexual violence would have been prosecuted as a sexual assault (or 'indecent assault' as it was then known) which had a lower maximum penalty. As the maximum penalty for rape under s.4 and aggravated sexual assault is life imprisonment, these reforms had the effect of elevating the seriousness of this type of sexual offending and equating it with the traditional offence of rape. Defilement of a child under the age of 15 criminalises a sexual act with a child.[47] Although the definition of this offence has been subject to legal reforms over the course of this study, the maximum penalty of life imprisonment has not changed.[48]

While there is a maximum term of life imprisonment for these offences, there is no minimum term. Mandatory minimum terms do not ordinarily form part of the Irish sentencing framework.[49] This means that the penalty can range from the lowest to the most severe penalty available in the State. There have been instances where suspended sentences have been imposed for the offence of rape[50] but a custodial sentence in a rape case is 'all but inescapable'.[51] In 2023, all rape offences resolved in the Central Criminal Court resulted in a term of imprisonment.[52] Nonetheless, such an extensive penalty range means that the role of the sentencing judge and how they exercise their discretion is of critical importance. A recent guidance judgement for the offence of rape was designed to assist in this regard, by setting out sentencing bands. Before considering this guidance for sexual offences, it is worthwhile reflecting on sentencing developments in other countries in order to situate Irish developments in the broader context.

The guidelines movement

As noted at the start of this chapter, the Supreme Court decision in *Tiernan* jettisoned the idea of the appellate courts developing sentencing guidance for specific offences, in part because of a lack of information on sentencing patterns. Unlike Ireland, many common law countries took steps during the latter stages of the twentieth century to address perceived sentencing disparity through various reforms aimed at limiting judicial discretion. This manifested itself in different ways but sentencing guidelines created by a statutory body has proven to be a popular approach. Since the establishment of the first sentencing commission in 1978 in Minnesota almost 50 different commissions have been 'proposed, established, disestablished or considered'.[53] The reason for the spread of the sentencing guidelines movement is contingent on a variety of dynamics specific to each country but can largely be sourced in a level of dissatisfaction with the existing sentencing situation and a perception that sentencing practice is inconsistent. Not all countries jumped on board with the sentencing guidelines trend. Some have rejected the idea of sentencing guidelines, reaffirming their commitment to the importance of discretion and the centrality of judges in sentencing outcomes. 'Success' is certainly not guaranteed, as there have been instances of sentencing commissions failing to launch guidelines or even being abolished before doing so.[54]

There are a number of different versions of guidelines but there are two main templates. There is a grid-based approach, associated with the US, which is frequently criticised for its rigidity and complexity.[55] Some argue that its mechanistic and dehumanising approach has contributed to an increase in punitive and harsh sentencing.[56] This system has not found popularity in other jurisdictions. Instead, many countries prefer the 'step-by-step' model often associated with England and Wales.[57] It is worthwhile explaining how this guideline model works in practice.

Using the offence of rape as an example, the guidelines in England and Wales provide a penalty range of four to 19 years for the offence, with life imprisonment possible as a maximum penalty. A departure from this range is possible but it requires the judge to give reasons for doing so. The guidelines establish three categories with separate starting points and ranges: category one (starting point: 15 years; range 13 to 19 years); category two (starting point: 10 years; range nine to 13 years); category three (starting point: seven years; range six to nine years).[58] To determine which starting point and category is appropriate, the judge should assess the culpability of the offender and the harm caused to the victim. There is a list of factors to guide judges in their assessment as to which category the offending falls within. The judge must also consider an additional list of aggravating and mitigating factors which may increase or decrease the sentence.

Although this sounds relatively straightforward, there are in fact nine steps to be followed in this process. These guidelines have been criticised for being complicated and rigid in their application.[59] Judges are required to follow these guidelines unless it would not be in the interests of justice to do so. Guidelines trump caselaw and, as a result, appellate court decisions are now only of illustrative value.[60] These guidelines are geared towards creating consistency of approach in decision-making. Taken in their totality, opponents to this model argue that the drive for consistency through the guideline mechanism can itself result in inconsistencies, particularly in exceptional or factually unusual cases. A model affording greater discretion could more accurately account for the individual factors that arise in a process that has always been centred on human rather than scientific assessment. In terms of the effect on sentencing outcomes, there has been an increase in sentence severity in England and Wales although research indicates that these increases cannot simply be attributed to the adoption of guidelines.[61] The introduction of mandatory minimum sentences for offences has been cited by some as a key cause of this sentencing inflation.[62] While guidelines may be on the horizon for Ireland, they have not arrived on these shores just yet. In the meantime, it is clear that Irish judges have departed from their resistance towards sentencing guidance and this is evident from a series of developments starting in the 2000s.

The Irish journey to guidance

There have been important developments in terms of judicial guidance over the last decade or so. In a way, these changes have happened somewhat organically rather than as a result of a deliberate or planned policy shift. The starting point began in the mid-2000s when a sentencing judge, dealing with a defendant convicted of rape, decided to examine patterns in sentences imposed by the Central Criminal Court (where rape cases are heard in Ireland) or reviewed on appeal from January 2005 to May 2007. His goal in doing so was to determine 'how long a period of imprisonment a perpetrator is required to serve and in what circumstances'.[63] Based on this analysis, Mr Justice Peter Charleton, the sentencing judge, identified sentencing bands indicating different levels of seriousness: lenient punishments; ordinary punishments; severe punishments; and condign punishments. Condign punishments referred to sentences of 15 years to life imprisonment. Given the shadow of the *Tiernan* decision, Mr Justice Charleton was careful to emphasise that it was not his intention to establish guidelines through conducting this important analysis.

The exercise highlighted the potential role sentencing information could play in bringing clarity, certainty and consistency to decision-making. Almost immediately, the Court of Criminal Appeal endorsed this approach, noting that the analysis was a 'valuable reference point' on the factors that can influence sentencing in rape cases.[64] The difficulty in building on this was a real lack of sentencing data or information systems in Ireland. The first steps taken in making progress on this issue came with the establishment of the Irish Sentencing Information System in the 2000s which produced a number of reports that provided important information on sentencing.[65] This project ultimately ran out of steam due to funding issues, but its work was continued, in some ways, by the Judicial Researchers Office (now the Research Support Office). Judges also have access to a sentencing handbook compiled under the supervision of the Judicial Studies Committee. In 2019, the Judicial Council's Sentencing Guidelines and Information Committee was established and this body has a statutory obligation to produce sentencing information.[66] It initially produced a report on the challenges in generating sentencing information in 2023 noting that there are 'profound' limitations in this regard.[67]

A significant shift in the appellate courts approach to guidance occurred in 2014.[68] Unexpectedly, the Court of Criminal Appeal issued sentencing guidance for firearms offences[69] and assault causing serious harm.[70] The Court noted that the *Tiernan* decision did not, in fact, preclude 'some broad level of guidance … as to the range of sentences which may be appropriate for an offence'.[71] These decisions made it clear that sentencing in an individual case remained a matter for the judge and that the guidance provided was not akin to creating a standardisation of penalty.[72] Since 2014, there has been a steady flow of judgments that have provided guidance on a range of offences. The Supreme Court endorsed this development and began to produce its own guidance decisions from 2019 onwards.[73]

There are two types of guidance that the appellate courts are currently willing to produce: formal and informal guidance. Formal guidance is based on taking a 'bottom-up' approach, meaning that the sentencing bands provided are usually reflective of a 'synthesis' of previous decisions.[74] This type of guidance is best described as a mirror rather than a lamp.[75] In other words, the guidance is reflective of existing and past practice in terms of sentencing for the particular offence under examination. It is not a new formulation developed by the appellate courts of what ought to happen in future cases (a 'top-down' or 'normative' approach). Informal guidance may be provided where the appellate court does not have sufficient sentencing data upon which to issue formal guidance but is willing to provide some general level of direction without getting into specifics.[76] There are two recent decisions on sexual offences that provide guidance that are relevant to this book so it is useful to examine these in more detail.

Guidance for sexual offences

In 2019, the Supreme Court produced formal guidance on the offence of rape and established sentencing bands indicative of different levels of seriousness.[77] The judgment was delivered by Mr Justice Peter Charleton, the same judge that took the initial step in 2007 to use information to create sentencing bands, now a member of the Supreme Court. The analysis of sentencing decisions in the 2007 case was heavily relied on in the 2019 judgment. The court established a ladder of seriousness through creating four sentencing bands to determine the headline sentence: 'below the norm' (less than four years); 'ordinary headline sentence' (seven years); more serious cases (ten to 15 years); and 'cases requiring up to life imprisonment' (from 15 years to life imprisonment). These bands relate to the assessment of the headline sentence only and mitigating factors should then be applied after determining the headline sentence.

The Supreme Court provided a non-exhaustive list of factors where a headline sentence of 15 years or more might be appropriate. These can broadly be divided into factors that relate to the level of violence and culpability of the offender, the relationship between the perpetrator and the victim, and the characteristics of the victim (see Table 2.1). The level of harm to the victim and the extent of the sexual and non-sexual violence involved forms a part of a number of these factors. The vulnerability of the victim, particularly through age, and the abuse of an inequity in the relationship between the victim and perpetrator, are significant aggravating factors. These are often more relevant in cases of child sexual abuse. The commission of a number of offences or prolonged periods of offending are seen as particularly aggravating. This arises in two types of scenarios. The perpetrator committed multiple offences during a single incident (see Chapter 4). Alternatively, the case may involve offences committed over an extended period of time against a victim or multiple victims (see Chapter 5). The guidance does not indicate the number or combination of factors required to result in a determination that a headline sentence of 15 years to life imprisonment is appropriate in an individual case. It is likely that such cases will involve multiple factors. For example, a case involving child sexual abuse will, at a minimum, include factors such as the harm to the victim and attacking the very young. This will be

Table 2.1: Factors in assessing a headline sentence of 15 years to life imprisonment in rape cases (*DPP v FE* [2019])

Levels of violence, culpability and harm caused	Relationship between perpetrator and victim	Characteristics of the victim
The harm done to the victim	Abusing a position of trust by a person in authority	Abusing a disparity in ages as between perpetrator or victims
Special violence and/or more than usual humiliation	Misusing a dominant position within a family	Abusing a particularly young or vulnerable victim
Victim is subjected to additional and gratuitous sexual perversions		Attacking the very young
Tricking a victim into a position of vulnerability		Attacking the very old
Coldly engaging in a campaign of rape		
Remorseless attitude not necessarily mitigated by later claims of repentance		
Participating in a gang-rape		
Using death threats		
Using implements of violence for the purpose of wielding authority or sexual perversion		

established by virtue of the crime itself prior to considering additional factors such as misusing a dominant position within the family. Of course, each individual case will always have a range of differing factors.

Given that guidance is based on existing and past practice as well as incorporating the principles of sentencing, it is unsurprising that many of the sentencing factors in the cases analysed in this study are identifiable in the guidance judgment and *vice versa*. There is a circularity here that may be effective in embedding sentencing factors and producing consistency in decision-making.

In 2021, the Court of Appeal also provided informal guidance on the offence of defilement of a child.[78] The court stated that there was insufficient sentencing data available to provide formal guidance. The court referenced the sentencing bands established in the Supreme Court case dealing with the offence of rape as being relevant to cases where the person was convicted of the offence of defilement of a child under the age of 15. The court also added an additional aggravating factor that increased culpability: recording and/or disseminating the recording of the crime. There is no specific guidance for rape under s.4 or aggravated sexual assault but it is fair to say that, given the similarities in terms of offence and penalty range, the guidance provided for rape is generally relevant and applicable to these offences also.

The purpose of these appellate judgments is to provide 'broad guidance as to the range of sentences that would ordinarily be appropriate for the offence in question across the spectrum'.[79] Sentencing judges may deviate from these bands in assessing the headline sentence. The appellate courts have acknowledged that there will be cases that arise that do not readily fit into any particular pattern.[80] The situation as originally articulated in *Tiernan*, that the appellate courts cannot impose a tariff or standardised penalty for sentencing courts to follow, still stands. While these guidance decisions provide a body of factors and information to sentencing judges in terms of the levels of seriousness within the penalty, discretion remains fundamental to sentencing decisions in Ireland. It is best to think of guidance judgments as a tool developed by the appellate courts for sentencing judges to assist in structuring their decision-making rather than a rigid format that must be followed. This distinguishes it from the situation in England and Wales and many other jurisdictions, where a more formalised system of guidelines has been in place for some time.

Conclusion

This chapter examined how judges sentence in practice while also taking a look at developments in sentencing from 1985 to the present situation. What is evident is that the discretion of sentencing judges operates within the confines of the proportionality principle, as developed through an ever-evolving 'sentencing canon' of judgments. The most important evolution in Irish sentencing practice has been the shift towards the issuance of sentencing guidance. These judgments set out sentencing bands reflective of the seriousness of the offence and detail the factors of relevance for each of these bands. The sentencing band of 15 years to life imprisonment is of the greatest interest here, as this book seeks to examine the factors that influence judges to impose a sentence of this severity in practice.

While the guidance judgments on sexual offences are informative in terms of factors relevant to each sentencing band, there is limited space in a Supreme Court judgment to provide a detailed analysis for each band. In the judgment establishing guidance for the offence of rape, a total of six paragraphs were dedicated to explaining the sentencing band for a headline sentence of 15 years to life imprisonment. This book attempts to fill in some of those gaps and expand on the analysis. Before examining the factors impacting sentence outcomes of this severity (Chapters 4 and 5), the next chapter takes a look at the sentencing choices of judges and deconstructs the component parts of these sentences. How the courts deal with a multi-crime offender is explored as well as the rules surrounding the imposition and administration of determinate and life sentences.

THREE

Deconstructing sentences

Introduction

Chapter 2 examined how sentencing works in practice and the principles that judges should apply when deliberating on what sentence to impose. There are also a range of legal rules, measures and orders that inform the selection and construction of a sentence by a judge. Given that the sentences under consideration here range from 15 years to life imprisonment, a judge must decide whether the sentence should be determinate (for example, 17 years' imprisonment) or indeterminate (for example, life imprisonment). A judge may decide to suspend a part of a custodial sentence to incentivise the rehabilitation and reintegration of the offender. They may add a post-release supervision order to the sentence to manage the risk of reoffending on release back into the community more effectively. Where a defendant has been convicted of multiple offences, a judge has to consider whether the sentences for each offence should run concurrently or consecutively.

The sentence selected and how it is constructed has a material impact on its meaning and the reality of time served in custody. This chapter deconstructs the different rules and judicial practices that impact sentencing judge's decisions to impose a lengthy determinate sentence or a life sentence. What is clear from the analysis is that judges were consistent in reserving sentences of this severity for multi-conviction cases. Before getting into this sentence analysis, an explanation of how this study worked, why it is important and the challenges it faced is useful context in understanding the findings presented in this and the following chapters.

How this study worked

As has already been stated, this book examines sentencing outcomes of 15 years to life imprisonment imposed for sexual offences from 1985 up to (and including) 2022. The cases (108)[1] were sourced through appellate judgments[2] and newspaper reporting.[3] In total, 279 documents were collected and these provided the material for this study. It was possible to source an appeal in over half of the cases (55 of 108) and these were often taken on the grounds that the sentence was too severe (or on occasion, too lenient) (46 of 55).[4] Considerable sections of the transcript from the sentencing hearing were cited or referred to in the judgments delivered by the appellate courts. The analysis of this material was supplemented with information from newspaper reports (both national and regional). Where the only documentary evidence for the case was derived from media reports, a policy of sourcing articles from different outlets was applied to increase the reliability of the case information.

A 93-item research instrument was utilised to extract information from all of the available sources identified for each case. The research took an expansive approach to factors that might influence the outcome including well-established sentencing factors (for example, aggravating and mitigating factors) as well as information on victim and defendant characteristics and the procedure of sentencing (see Table 3.1). Mining the available documentary evidence for as much information as possible allows for an exploration of sentencing practice in a way that has not previously been produced (at least in Ireland). Of course, focusing on factors to understand sentencing outcomes can tend to simplify decision-making.[5] The idea that a certain number or combination of factors result in a certain type of sentence outcome downplays the tendency for judges to look at the 'whole offence story'.[6] Rather than solely presenting a catalogue of factors, this study attempts to construct a picture of the multitude of influences that may be impacting sentence outcomes.

Criminologists interested in understanding sentencing often analyse decision-making through employing the 'focal concerns' framework, namely that judges are primarily concerned with culpability and blameworthiness, community safety and the practical consequences of the sentencing outcome.[7] For example, some concentrate on analysing disparities in sentencing through focusing on the impact of defendant characteristics.[8] These quantitative studies frequently rely on rich data generated by sentencing commissions which require judges to provide a detailed rationale when sentencing.[9] Focusing on specific factors at case level may not capture the myriad influences on judicial decision-making. In any event, this data is simply not available in Ireland. Legal scholars tend to scrutinise sentencing principles and policy developed at the appellate level as well as legislative change. Sentencing judges are bound to follow the legal precedent established in previous cases decided on appeal. The focus of legal scholars on judgments of the appellate courts can provide valuable insight into the principles of sentencing but this sheds little light on what is happening in practice. We also know very little about how, and in what way, the principles and guidance developed by the appellate courts impacts sentencing practice at trial level.[10] This book tries to marry the legal and criminological perspectives using the available resources to provide some fresh insight.

Qualitative techniques are employed to examine decisions at trial level while also tracing these decisions through the appellate process. It is important to understand the impact of

Table 3.1: Data extracted from available sentencing sources (sample)

Sentence information	**Data on victim and offender**	**Rationale for sentence**	**The appeal process**
Length of sentence	Age	Level of seriousness	Nature of appeal application
Headline sentence	Gender	Totality of offending	Decision of appellate court
Principal offence	Nationality	Aggravating factors specific to sexual offences	Length of increase/decrease of sentence
Single or multiple offences	Evidence of co-accused	General aggravating factors	Level of seriousness
Total number offences	Number of victims	Risk of reoffending	Assessment of aggravating factors
Number of incidents	Relationship between the parties	Previous criminal history	Assessment of mitigating factors
Length of victimisation	Location of offending	Mitigating factors	Influence of public protection
Concurrent or consecutive sentences			Influence of guilty plea
Suspension or part suspension			Influence of previous criminal history
Full or sample charges			
Post-release supervision orders			
Plea of accused			
Level of guilty plea discount			
Victim impact statement			
Evidence of delay			

the appellate process on sentence outcomes in the individual case as well as the impact of these appellate decisions on future cases. The role of judges, their institutional environment and diverse array of influences are also significant factors in decision-making and these are explored in Chapter 6. The study provides valuable insights into how judges apply legal rules in difficult cases to arrive at an outcome that has to reflect a multitude of interests. The consistencies and disparities evident in this decision-making process are highlighted and their meaning interrogated.

It is necessary to acknowledge the limitations of this research and these primarily relate to the source material. Of course, the most reliable source of information would be the sentencing remarks of judges but there are major, perhaps insurmountable, barriers to gaining access to the sentencing remarks for the period under review. Sentencing remarks are not ordinarily published. A system of audio recording (called 'Digital Audio Recording' or 'DAR') of court proceedings has been in place since the 2010s but these recordings are not publicly available. For decisions preceding this, an audio record does not exist. Legislation requires that sexual offence cases (including sentencing hearings) be held *in camera* (or in the absence of the public) to protect the anonymity of the victim.[11] This presents significant issues in terms of gaining ethical access to this type of data through court transcripts or audio recordings. Some studies in Ireland have gained valuable access to rape case files at various stages of the criminal process although the time period under review was limited and these studies did not tend to focus on sentencing.[12] O'Malley conducted an analysis of sentencing patterns in sexual offence cases that provided valuable information and insight into general sentencing factors.[13] An analysis conducted by the Judicial Researchers' Office on sentencing in rape cases also relied principally on appellate judgments and newspaper reports, with occasional use of digital audio recordings.[14] This report and its subsequent iterations are no longer publicly accessible.

Reliance on newspaper reporting can be viewed as problematic as certain types of cases may be over-represented in the media and there is also potential for bias within the reporting.[15] O'Connell notes a bias in the Irish media towards the reporting of violent and sensational crimes.[16] While this practice may be viewed negatively in terms of its impact on shaping public opinion of crime, it was useful in the context of a study focused on a country with a small population. It meant that there was a very high probability that all serious sexual offence cases were reported in the media. This increased the likelihood of capturing the majority of these decisions although this is not verifiable due to the lack of comparable official data.

All cases in this study were reported in the national and local press. Healy and O'Donnell note the value of using newspaper reporting to explore sentencing patterns where official data is limited or lacking.[17] In addition, the extensive media coverage throughout the trial, sentencing and appellate process provided important information for analysis. Having analysed 108 decisions, it is clear that the court reports produced by journalists are very detailed and great efforts have been made to record the offences committed, the sentence outcome and the reasons for that outcome. In the absence of the availability of official data and records, it is the media that have documented these decisions and without which this study would not have been possible.

There is a hierarchy of reliability in terms of the information extracted from the available sources. Data on sentence information, the victim and defendant, the facts of the case and the appeal process can be treated as reliable. The rationale for the sentence is much more difficult in terms of reliability, particularly where the analysis is dependent on newspaper reporting. Even with a full transcript of sentencing remarks, providing a complete analysis of the rationale for a sentence is fraught with difficulty. The 'quest to uncover the "real" reason behind decision making' in sentencing is challenging as the articulation of reasons will rarely reflect reality.[18] As such, the findings in this study are best understood as giving some (but not a full) insight into the factors influencing sentencing in serious sexual offence cases. The methodology employed in this study may provide a stepping-stone for future research in the area.

The multi-conviction conundrum

Defendants were overwhelmingly being sentenced for committing multiple offences, with 94.4 per cent of cases involving more than one offence.[19] In some cases, multiple offences were committed during the course of a single incident. In others, often involving child sexual abuse, the offender was convicted of multiple offences arising from multiple incidents against multiple victims over a significant period of time (see Chapters 4 and 5). The issue of how to deal with (and justify the approach to) sentencing where multiple offences have been committed and are being dealt with at the same hearing has been described as a 'sleeper' problem for many countries.[20] The multi-conviction offender can effectively benefit from a 'bulk' discount by virtue of all of the offences being considered at the same sentencing hearing.[21]

In serious sexual offence cases, the offences being dealt with at the sentencing hearing were, at times, an underestimation of the volume of offending. In one third of cases, only a sample of the initial charges were brought forward by the Director of Public Prosecutions (the DPP). The guidelines for prosecutors state that where there are a large number of similar offences it is recommended that a sample of representative counts should be 'carefully considered' as too many counts may complicate the trial process.[22] These guidelines advise prosecutors of the importance in balancing the requirement to reflect the totality of the offending while, at the same time, not overloading the indictment. For example, in a case involving the sexual abuse of three children over a period of six years, there were originally 400 charges. The offender was convicted of a sample of these charges following a guilty plea. In Ireland, when an offender has been convicted of multiple offences and they are being dealt with at the same sentencing hearing, it is considered best practice for the judge to impose an individual sentence for each offence.[23] Once the judge has completed this task, a critical decision arises – whether these sentences should run concurrently or consecutively.

If the sentences are imposed concurrently, the offender will serve the term of imprisonment that is the longest across all offences. This will be the sentence for the most serious offence or 'principal offence'. Take the following example as an illustration. A defendant is convicted of one count of rape, one count of sexual assault and one count of false imprisonment arising from a single incident. The judge sentences the defendant to 15 years' imprisonment for the rape offence, three years for sexual assault and two years for false imprisonment. The judge orders that these sentences are to run concurrently. As a consequence, the defendant will effectively serve a 15-year sentence. If the judge decides that the sentences should run consecutively, the total sentence would be 20 years (15 plus 3 plus 2), as these sentences would run one after the other. The difficulty with imposing consecutive sentences is that it can result in a sentence length that is at odds with the general limitations of sentencing policy and practice. For instance, 20 years imprisonment is close to what a person sentenced to life imprisonment is likely to serve prior to release back into the community.[24]

When deliberating on the sentencing, a judge may decide to impose some sentences concurrently and others consecutively. Although not the preferred approach, it is also possible for a judge to select a global headline sentence reflective of the offending as a whole before working backwards to determine the headline sentence for each individual offence. The sentencing judge must ensure that the combination of these individual sentences reflect the global headline sentence.[25] Critically, in order to ensure that the offender receives a sentence that is proportionate to the gravity of the offending in the case as a whole, the court should consider the totality of offending and make adjustments to the sentence outcome accordingly. This rule applies irrespective of how the sentence is formulated. The following examines the practice, policy and principles shaping sentence outcomes in multi-conviction cases.

Concurrent or consecutive sentences

Judges imposed concurrent sentences in 86.2 per cent of multi-conviction cases.[26] In making this decision, judges are guided by principle and practice, although there are no 'hard and fast' legal rules on this.[27] There is a presumption that sentences will be imposed concurrently and this is particularly the case where the offending related to a single incident.[28] The appellate courts have stated that consecutive sentences may be imposed where there is a gap in offending, there is more than one victim or the facts for each offence are unrelated.[29] If there are multiple victims in a sexual offence case, it is now an error of principle for a sentencing judge to fail to consider consecutive sentences.[30]

The judicial policy that consecutive sentences should be imposed sparingly relates to the risk that this may result in an excessively long overall sentence and this would be a disproportionate outcome.[31] But the opposite may also be true. A multi-crime offender can benefit from a significant discount as a result of the sentences being ordered to run concurrently.[32] This is particularly the case when there is a large volume of offences before the court for sentencing, as is evident in many of the serious sexual offence cases in this study. Judges are tasked with finding some kind of balance and the multiplicity of offending is clearly a significant driving factor influencing the selection of a sentence outcome of 15 years or more.

In the rare instances where consecutive sentences were imposed, the defendant was often convicted of multiple offences arising from multiple incidents involving multiple victims. These cases usually involved a combination of consecutive and concurrent sentences. The reason for imposing consecutive sentences related to the importance of reflecting the harm caused to each individual victim. This is best illustrated through sentencing remarks that were approved on appeal:

> To impose one sentence in respect of the offences against one victim and then impose concurrent sentences in respect of the other offences, would inevitably suggest to the second and third victims that the offences against them were of less importance, or indeed of no real importance, and that the convicted person would not really be serving any sentence in respect of the offences committed against them.[33]

It is important to note that concurrent sentences were imposed in many cases where there were multiple incidents with multiple victims. Consecutive sentences in these types of cases were the exception not the rule.

The totality principle

The totality principle also influences the sentencing outcome in multi-conviction cases. The purpose of this principle is to minimise disproportionalities and disparities in sentencing. The foundation of the principle is that when sentencing for multiple offences, the judge should take an aggregate view of the total sentence outcome to ensure that it is reflective of the offending as a whole. During this assessment, the judge may alter the sentence upwards or downwards to make sure that it is proportionate and fair.[34] The optimal approach is that once sentencing for each offence has been carried out, the judge should then reflect on the offending in the round and may choose to adjust the overall sentence accordingly.[35] When imposing consecutive sentences, the judge must consider the sentence outcome in its global terms. Adjusting a sentence should only be considered if the existing outcome is disproportionate or to avoid a 'crushing sentence'.[36]

The totality principle should also be applied where concurrent sentences are being imposed. Given the volume of offending in some cases, it might appear that ordering the sentences to run concurrently cannot accurately reflect the breadth of the offending in an individual case. To address this, the principle permits the sentencing judge to adjust the sentence for the principal offence upwards to reflect 'the particular gravity of all the circumstances of offending'.[37] So, for example, in a case where multiple offences have been committed the judge may impose a sentence for the principal offence that is greater than what would have been imposed had they been sentencing for that singular offence alone. That sentence should then be interpreted as reflecting the totality of offending before the court rather than simply the outcome for that individual offence.

Whether the sentences imposed are adequate in light of the volume of offending in these cases is something that may attract legitimate debate. What is clear is that when interpreting long-term imprisonment in sexual offence cases, the multi-crime component and the manner by which the courts deal with this issue is critical in understanding the sentencing outcome. In their deliberations, judges must also decide whether to impose a determinate sentence or a sentence of life imprisonment. This selection has different limitations and implications which will now be explored.

Determinate sentences

A range of 15 years to life imprisonment includes options of both determinate and indeterminate sentences. In this study, the majority of sentences (80 per cent or 86 of 108) were determinate in nature, in the sense that a sentencing judge set a numerical value on the custodial sentence. From this, it is possible to calculate a date of release from custody with a good degree of certainty. Once released, those who serve determinate sentences are not subject to any supervision conditions in the community unless a measure, such as a post-release supervision order, has been imposed.

In theory, a period that spans from 15 years to life imprisonment provides an infinite number of years that could be selected by judges. The analysis in this study demonstrates that there are limitations in terms of the length of sentence that judges are willing to impose. In over half of all determinate sentence cases, the most frequently selected outcome was 15 years' imprisonment (53.5 per cent or 46 of 86). The remaining cases ranged from greater than 15 years up to (and including) 20 years imprisonment (37.2 per cent or 32 of 86). There were only a small number of cases that exceeded 20 years (9.3 per cent or 8 of 86) and this was sometimes as a result of consecutive sentences being imposed.

In some countries it is possible to impose very lengthy determinate sentences such that the term of imprisonment may exceed the life span of the individual. The practical effect of this is that a determinate sentence may end up being a *de facto* life sentence or the equivalent of a whole life sentence.[38] This is not a practice that is evident in Ireland. In fact, judicial policy and practice appears to limit determinate sentences to 20 years' imprisonment, with little deviation above this threshold. A Supreme Court decision that established guidance for assault manslaughter cases set a determinate headline sentencing band of 15 to 20 years' imprisonment for offending of the worst culpability.[39] The court stated that in exceptional cases a life sentence may be imposed. This indicates that the appellate courts see 20 years as a general threshold in terms of the length of a determinate sentence, with the next step up in severity being a life sentence. There are exceptions to this but they are rare. The position was summed up by one sentencing judge who expressed an inclination to impose a 30-year sentence but stated that to do so and claim that the sentence was less than a life sentence would be 'judicially dishonest and populist'.[40] Indeed, the average time served by life sentence prisoners that have been released back into the community is around 19 years.[41] Life imprisonment is the 'ultimate penalty' and the most severe penalty available in the State.[42] As such, life imprisonment acts as the 'benchmark of severity' by which other determinate penalties for less serious offending is established.[43] Sentencing deliberations may also be anchored by outcomes in previous cases. For example, it is possible that the sentence in *Tiernan* of 21 years, subsequently reduced by the Supreme Court to 17 years on appeal, had an anchoring effect on subsequent deliberations in cases of similar seriousness.[44] A sentence of this length was exceptional in the 1980s and judges may have treated this as a benchmark for determinate sentence outcomes.

The sentences of 15 years or more included in this study are based on the sentence outcome prior to consideration of additional orders that may have been applied. The sentence outcome is different from the headline sentence. The headline sentence is the sentence arrived at following the assessment of the gravity of the offence but prior to applying any mitigating factors. It was only possible to identify a headline sentence in just over one third of determinate sentence cases (36.1 per cent or 31 of 86). Sentencing guidance judgments are directed at the calculation of a headline sentence only. Mitigation is applied separately and this then leads to the sentence outcome. A judge, when imposing a sentence, may also make additional orders such as suspending a part of the sentence. The sentence outcome in this study is reflective of the sentence after accounting for mitigation but without calculation of a part suspension or additional order. To take an example, a sentencing judge decides that the appropriate headline sentence is 20 years but mitigating factors reduces the sentence by five years, resulting in a final sentence outcome of 15 years. The judge then decides to suspend three years of the sentence on the basis that the offender comply with a 10-year post-release supervision order to minimise the risk to the community. The effective carceral component is now a 12-year custodial sentence (minus remission of 25 per cent). This is conditional on compliance with the community supervision order. It is useful to bear all this in mind when reading this book.

Suspending a part of the sentence

In understanding the meaning of a determinate sentence, it is important to be cognisant of whether the judge ordered a part of the sentence to be suspended. Part suspension was evident in just over half of the cases (52.3 per cent) where a determinate sentence was imposed.[45] The period of suspension in these cases ranged from one to nine years. The effect of this is to reduce the sentence served in real terms, assuming the offender complies with the conditions of the suspension. The part suspension of a sentence is a long-established practice which was given a statutory framework in 2006.[46] There is no limit on the term of imprisonment that may be suspended. The suspension is contingent on the defendant complying with the conditions established in statute and by the court.[47] This will include keeping the peace and being of good behaviour. The court may specify that the offender be placed under the supervision of the Probation Service for the purpose of rehabilitation and/or public protection. The offender might be required to undergo treatment for drug, alcohol or substance use, engage in education or training or participate in psychological counselling or treatment. The rate of part suspension is higher than what is evident when examining recent rape cases. In 2023, the Central Criminal Court suspended a part of the sentence in 40 per cent of rape offences resulting in a sentence of imprisonment.[48]

Post-release supervision orders

Sex offenders may be subject to notification and supervision orders on release in addition to their custodial sentence.[49] These were created *via* legislation in 2001 and may be imposed at the discretion of the sentencing judge. All persons convicted of a sexual offence are subject to notification requirements on release back into the community.[50] In addition, a judge may impose a post-release supervision order with additional conditions. From 2001 to 2022, it was possible to identify a post-release supervision order in 38.5 per cent of the cases where a determinate sentence was imposed.[51] It may be the case that there were orders made in additional cases but this was not identifiable from the available source material. The period of supervision in the community imposed by judges ranged from one to 12 years. Given that determinate sentence prisoners are not subject to supervision on release, these orders were employed by judges in cases where there was a perception that the offender was at a risk of reoffending and supervision in the community could assist in ameliorating that risk.

It was often the case that a judge would suspend a part of the sentence and then impose a post-release supervision order as a condition of the part suspension. For example, in one case a sentence of life imprisonment was reduced to a determinate sentence on appeal based primarily on the need to properly account for the guilty plea. The court was of the view that the offender posed a danger to the public. Imposing a determinate sentence rather than a life sentence would mean that the offender would no longer be the subject of the parole decision-making process and would not be monitored in the community to the same extent. Supervision was something the court viewed as necessary and, to address this, the court suspended two and a half years of the determinate sentence and imposed a ten-year post-release supervision order as a condition of that part suspension. The court specified that the defendant must receive psychological counselling and comply with the directions of the Probation Service. Failure to comply with this would mean that the offender would be required to serve the suspended part of the sentence in custody. As these orders apply specifically to sex offenders and are selectively imposed by judges in individual cases, they constitute an additional penalty to the custodial sentence.[52]

Remission

Determinate sentence prisoners will typically receive 25 per cent remission on their sentence for good behaviour.[53] An offender sentenced to 20 years can expect to serve 15 years in custody after accounting for remission. This is not a guaranteed legal right but is seen as standard practice and for the 'prisoner to lose'.[54] Remission forms part of the administration of the sentence governed by the executive and a sentencing judge has no role in relation to the application of this policy. Remission does not come with any conditions of supervision by the Probation Service. A prisoner may qualify for additional remission (of up to one third of their sentence) where they have demonstrated good conduct through engaging in rehabilitative activities that reduce risk. Sex offenders are unlikely to be able to access this added level of remission as it does not appear that prisoners convicted of a sexual offence have been granted this level of remission in practice.[55] The Minister for Justice may also grant temporary release to prisoners to assist in the rehabilitation of the offender, on humanitarian grounds or to relieve prison overcrowding.[56] Sentence-specific data on temporary release for sex offenders is not available but the Department of Justice has indicated that only low-risk sex offenders will be permitted temporary release and even in such cases it is unlikely.[57]

Taking all of these different elements of determinate sentencing into consideration, there are components that may reduce the time served in custody, such as the part suspension of a sentence and remission. But there are also measures, such as a post-release supervision order, that may serve an important function in imposing community supervision requirements that support the interest in public protection. The need to minimise and control risk certainly played some role in the selection of life imprisonment as a sentence and this is now discussed in more detail.

Life imprisonment

In 20 per cent of cases (22 of 108) a judge selected to impose a sentence of life imprisonment. This is noteworthy as, at least in European countries, it is exceptional for any defendant to be sentenced to life imprisonment for offences outside of those in the homicide category.[58] In Ireland, aside from the mandatory life sentence for murder, there are an additional 25 offences where life imprisonment may be imposed as a maximum penalty, five of which relate to sexual offences.[59] In practice, a discretionary sentence of life imprisonment is rare and recent research showed that it is reserved primarily for serious sexual offences.[60] In this study, multiple life sentences were frequently imposed in individual cases and while a sexual offence may have been the 'principal' offence, additional sentences of life imprisonment were occasionally imposed for other offences. For example, in one case a defendant was sentenced to eight concurrent life sentences for sexual offences (6), false imprisonment (1) and aggravated burglary (1).

Although judicial discretion in Ireland may be wider than many other sentencing systems, judges have been strongly encouraged by the appellate courts to opt for a determinate sentence, even in cases where the offending warrants a life sentence. The rationale for this is that it is unsatisfactory for a court, in exercising its sentencing powers, not to know the period of imprisonment that the person will serve.[61] To justify the imposition of a life sentence the offending must 'not only be of a very serious type … but be so in an exceptional way'.[62] Adding this to the general principles that shape sentencing practice (particularly the requirement to apply a reduction for mitigating factors) means that the likelihood of life imprisonment being the outcome is a remote prospect even in the most serious of cases.

A life sentence is a qualitatively different choice to a determinate sentence. In terms of how life imprisonment operates in practice, the sentence does not ordinarily mean life in prison. Since 2019, a life sentence prisoner is required, by legislation, to serve a minimum term of 12 years in prison before becoming eligible for review by a statutory Parole Board.[63] Prior to this, there was a policy that the interim Parole Board would not review a life sentence prisoner until a minimum of seven years had been served in custody. The decision as to whether a life sentence prisoner was released, and at what point, was the responsibility of the Minister for Justice. The Minister was advised by the interim Parole Board and largely accepted the Board's recommendations.[64] Although life sentence prisoners are entitled to have their sentence reviewed at a certain point, release is not guaranteed. The average time served by life sentence prisoners released back in the community has increased over the course of this study (from 12 years (1985 to 1994) to 19 years (2008 to 2017)).[65] These figures only provide the average time served of those released. In 2019, 5 per cent of the prisoners in custody serving life sentences for homicide had spent 30 years or more in prison.[66] Unlike determinate sentenced prisoners, if released, life sentence prisoners are placed under the supervision of the Probation Service for the remainder of their lives. If they breach their conditions of release, they may be recalled to prison.

Sentencing judges are not involved in the decision to release a life sentence prisoner nor can they impose a minimum term to be served prior to being considered for release. Remission does not apply to a life sentence nor is it possible to suspend a part of the sentence. In order to secure release, a life sentence prisoner must engage with the parole process and meet the requirements of the Parole Board. The Parole Board may make a parole order for release where an applicant does not present 'an undue risk to the safety and security of members of the public', has been rehabilitated, is capable of reintegrating into society on release and it is appropriate in all circumstances to do so.[67] As will become evident from the analysis of life imprisonment and risk, the qualitatively different components of this sentence appear to play some part in its selection.

The risk factor

The selection of life imprisonment as a penalty is contingent on an assessment by the judge that the offending is of an exceptionally serious nature. An analysis of sentencing remarks in these cases also gives insight into how the risk of reoffending may be a contributing factor in choosing an indeterminate sentence. In sentencing remarks, judges stated that offenders were a 'menace to society',[68] that there was a 'duty to protect the people of Ireland'[69] as well as a need to protect specific categories of victims – 'protect women, protect prostitutes'.[70] Perceptions of dangerousness were at times informed by evidence or reports provided by experts in risk assessment. One judge referenced a Probation Officer report that stated the offender posed a risk to young women and that custody did not appear to be a deterrent. In 15 of the 22 cases, the previous criminal history of the defendant was highlighted and contributed to the judges' risk assessment. Judges noted that 'the nature of the previous offending indicates that the offender represents a continuing danger to the public'[71] and expressed concern that there was a 'proclivity to rape … again'.[72] There were four cases where the offender had prior convictions for rape. In one case, the defendant had previously been convicted of the rape of a teenage girl as well as the manslaughter of his father. The sentencing judge described the defendant as a 'highly dangerous man whose threat to society is ongoing'.[73]

There was evidence that the indeterminate nature of life imprisonment was viewed by some judges as an instrument that could control, to a certain degree, the future risk of reoffending. Sentencing judges appeared to take some comfort in the fact that the Parole Board would make a decision as to whether the offender should be released back into the community or further detained. As one judge noted, release is not a given and is based on whether, and if, the offender is 'safe to be released'.[74] Judges also noted that as a result of life imprisonment the defendant would be subject to 'rigorous supervision' on release, could be precluded from visiting areas where the victim resides and would be 'subject to recall' for breach of any of his conditions of release.[75] The Parole Board's decision-making has been described as risk averse and cautious.[76] Ultimately, a life sentence prisoner will not be released unless they are at a low risk of reoffending.[77] Sentencing judges are aware of the different consequences of imposing a life sentence over a determinate sentence.

The inclusion of risk references in sentencing remarks raises potential legal issues. Incorporating considerations of risk, dangerousness or anything akin to preventative detention in legal decision-making presents specific issues of compatibility with *Bunreacht na hÉireann* (the Irish Constitution).[78] The basic issue being that a person should only be punished for the crimes they have committed and not for potential future crimes that they have not yet contemplated (and may never commit). The Supreme Court has stated that the sentence of life imprisonment itself is 'wholly punitive' and it does not incorporate any component of preventative detention.[79] Judgments of the appellate courts have established that a sentencing judge cannot explicitly employ evidence of a risk of reoffending or dangerousness to increase the sentence. However, a judge may incorporate considerations of preventative detention as long as this is within the confines of a proportionate sentence.[80] To put it another way, if the offending warrants a life sentence, and this outcome could potentially be imposed in factually similar cases, then it is likely that the sentence will be viewed as proportionate irrespective of the input on the issue of risk and dangerousness.

At times, there are cases that come before the courts where the offender has committed serious offences and there is a consensus among criminal justice professionals and experts that they are at a high risk of reoffending at a serious level. This creates a real and practical problem for sentencing judges. In this context, a subsequent parole decision-making process determining release is perceived as valuable in ensuring that the risk level is lowered prior to release. Yet, imposing a life sentence on this basis creates compatibility issues with the principle of proportionality. The question as to whether the life sentence amounts to preventative detention has been the subject of a number of appeals. The appellate courts have tended to give sentencing judges significant leeway where the risk of reoffending is connected to the rationale for imposing life imprisonment in sentencing remarks. These types of remarks have been characterised as incidental and do 'not exceed what is required for purely penal purposes in so aggravated a case'.[81] It is still difficult to discern when a sentencing judge will be deemed to have overstepped the mark on this issue of risk. Given the seriousness of the offending in the cases in this study, a sentence of life imprisonment is certainly legally defensible based on existing principles.

Conclusion

This chapter examined the sentences selected by judges and the meaning of those sentences. The multiplicity of offending is a significant factor that influenced long-term imprisonment for sexual offences. As such, the sentence outcome needs to be interpreted as being reflective of the totality of offending in multi-offence cases. Judges were tasked with attempting to reflect the sheer volume of offending in the sentence outcome while operating within the numerical limitations set out in principle and practice for determinate sentences. The lack of community supervision requirements in a determinate sentence motivated some judges to impose a post-release supervision order in an attempt to manage and control risk to the community on release. The imposition of a life sentence means that release from custody is dictated by a subsequent decision-making process and on release, the offender remains under supervision for the rest of their lives. These differences may be a motivating factor in the selection of this sentence over a determinate sentence, particularly where the defendant is perceived to be at a high risk of reoffending. Having deconstructed these sentences to better understand their meaning, the following two chapters examine cases where the defendant is being sentenced for crimes committed against adult victims (Chapter 4) and crimes of child sexual abuse (Chapter 5).

FOUR

Sentencing crimes committed against adult victims

Introduction

In cases where the victim of the offending was an adult, a very specific and consistent fact pattern emerged. The perpetrators of these crimes were all male and the victims were all female. The perpetrator was a stranger or a very recent acquaintance of the victim. The offending often occurred in a public place. The cases primarily involved a single incident but multiple offences were committed during this incident. The use of weapons and death threats was frequently evident in these cases. Over two thirds of offenders had a previous criminal history, with prior convictions for sexual offences featuring prominently. In terms of mitigation, many offenders did plead guilty but, aside from this, there was little evidence of offence-related or personal mitigation.

Of the 108 cases included in this study, 45 involved crimes committed against adult victims. In this chapter, sentencing judge's assessments of the gravity of the offence, the culpability of the offender and the harm caused to the victim(s) will be explored. The influence of factors relating to the offender, such as their previous criminal history and the perceived risk of reoffending proved to be relevant in sentence deliberations. The challenge in applying a reduction in sentence arising from mitigating factors, such as the guilty plea, in cases of such seriousness is also considered. Focusing on specific factors is important and illuminative but diving into the details can sometimes obscure the bigger picture. Taken as a whole, many of these cases appear to reflect some parallels with a cultural (and prejudicial) belief that rape is often committed by a stranger in a public place causing physical injury. These beliefs are known as 'rape myths' and this chapter concludes with a discussion on whether these myths play a role in sentence selection.

Offences and sentences

The principal offences which defendants were convicted of were the offences of rape or rape under s.4 (91.1 per cent or 41 of 45). The remaining defendants were convicted of aggravated sexual assault (6.7 per cent or three of 45) or aiding and abetting a rape (2.2 per cent or one of 45) as the principal offence. Offenders were convicted of multiple offences in 86.7 per cent (39 of 45) of cases and where there was more than one conviction, the number of offences ranged from two to 13. Of the defendants where there were multiple offences, almost all of them (87.2 per cent or 34 of 39) involved additional sexual offences. Many of these additional offences were serious in nature and included rape, rape under s.4, aggravated sexual assault and sexual assault. There were also cases where the defendant was being sentenced for non-sexual offences. False imprisonment, assault, burglary, robbery and threats to kill were offences evident across a number of these cases.

Such was the seriousness of the offending, that in 41.2 per cent (14 of 34) of cases where multiple sentences were imposed for sexual offences, the sentence length for what might be described as the 'principal' offence was replicated across the sentences for the additional offences. So, for example, a judge would impose 15 years' imprisonment for each of the three rape offences and order that these sentences run concurrently. As such, the use of the term 'principal offence' is a bit of a misnomer here as the sentencing judge did not consider these offences as secondary. The offences committed during the incident were deemed of equal seriousness and this was indicated in the sentence length imposed for each individual offence. A small number of offenders were sentenced for a single offence (13.3 per cent or 6 of 45).

Where there were multiple offences, sentences were imposed concurrently in most cases (82.1 per cent or 32 of 39). Where consecutive sentences were imposed, the cases involved multiple victims but it is important to note that many cases involving multiple victims did not result in consecutive sentences. Whether concurrent or consecutive, the sentence outcome can be considered as reflective of the judges' perspective on the totality of the offending in the case. Judges partly suspended the sentence imposed in 40 per cent of determinate sentence cases (14 of 35), with the period of suspension ranging from one to nine years. Since 2001, it was possible to identify a post-release supervision order in 34.6 per cent of determinate sentence cases (9 of 26) ranging from a period of 18 months to 12 years. It was evident from sentencing remarks that there was a correlation between an assessment that the offender posed a risk of reoffending and the use of a post-release supervision order. In all but one of these cases the sentencing judge specifically identified the need to protect the public in their sentencing remarks when imposing such an order.

As outlined in Chapter 3, judges frequently selected either 15 years or life imprisonment when imposing a sentence and this is evident in cases involving adult victims (15 years = 35.6 per cent or 16 of 45 and life imprisonment = 22.2 per cent or 10 of 45). Outside of these choices, most sentences imposed were greater than 15 years and up to (and including) 20 years (28.9 per cent or 13 of 45). There were only six cases (or 13.3 per cent) where a sentence of more than 20 years was imposed.

In terms of the use of long-term imprisonment over the decades covered in this study, it does appear that penalties ranging from 15 years to life imprisonment are being imposed more frequently by the courts. Just under one third of these sentences were imposed in the first half of the study (1985 to 2003 – 31.1 per cent or 14 of 45) with just over two thirds of cases imposed in the latter half of the study (2004 to 2022 – 68.9 per cent or 31 of 45). Of course, there are many factors that may influence sentencing patterns at any given time and bearing in mind the small number and exceptional nature of the offending, it would not be wise to draw any conclusions from this in terms of assertions of increased punitiveness. Nonetheless, it is worthwhile noting the more frequent use of the upper end of the penalty range.

The gravity of the offence

As outlined in Chapter 2, sentencing judges are required to apply the principle of proportionality, the first step of which is to assess the gravity of the offence. This includes an assessment of the harm caused, the culpability of the offender, as well as incorporating any aggravating factors that arise in the case. Judges are also guided by the decision of the Supreme Court in *FE*, which provided information on factors that might warrant a term of imprisonment of 15 years or more. Although this decision was issued in 2019, and therefore comes after many of these sentencing decisions were made, the guidance provided was formulated based on the previous decisions of the sentencing courts and the appellate courts. As a result, it is reflective of past practice and provides an instructive tool in understanding the relevant sentencing factors.

By virtue of the sentence outcome alone, it is clear that these cases represent the most serious offending within the penalty range. An examination of sentencing remarks indicates that judges explicitly stated that the offending behaviour was at the upper range of the penalty or at the most serious level.[1]

Sentencing judges did not always use the language of 'upper range', 'very serious' or 'exceptional' that is articulated in the judgments of the Court of Appeal or the Supreme Court. Nonetheless, the language employed to describe the offending in sentencing remarks can clearly be equated with an assessment that it was of the highest level of seriousness. Sentencing remarks on the gravity of the offence(s) included phrases such as: 'utmost seriousness';[2] 'truly horrific';[3] 'most terrible';[4] 'beggars belief';[5] 'despicable';[6] 'horrendous';[7] 'abominable';[8] and 'barbaric'.[9] This language, while useful in illustrating the extremity of violence, can only give so much insight. The following provides a more detailed examination of key factors relevant to the judicial assessment of offence seriousness.

The multiplicity of offending

For the most part, these cases involved a single incident (84.4 per cent or 38 of 45) but these single incidents involved the commission of multiple offences (see Table 4.1). Over one third of cases involved multiple victims (37.7 per cent or 17 of 45). Judges noted the prolonged nature of the criminal event(s) as particularly aggravating. In one case, the court stated that one of the incidents lasted two hours and 40 minutes. In another, there were two victims (the defendant's partner and her mother) who were subjected to the offences of rape, sexual assault and false imprisonment that were perpetrated over a number of days. In cases where the offender has been convicted of a number of offences arising from the same criminal event, the Supreme Court has stated that 'all of these offences inform the

Table 4.1: Incidents and victims in sexual offence cases (adult victims)

	Single victim	**Multiple victims**
Single incident	27 60%	11 24.5%
Multiple incidents	1 2.2%	6 13.3%

seriousness of each … crime' and this is evident in the approach adopted by judges in assessing the totality of the offending.[10]

There were some cases where the defendant was being sentenced for more than one incident where sexual offences were committed (15.5 per cent or 7 of 45) and these incidents usually involved different victims (six of seven). Multiple incidents and multiple victims are aggravating factors that will impact the sentence outcome.[11] In one instance, an offender was sentenced to 18.5 years imprisonment having attacked three women on three different occasions over a period of five years. There were also cases where offences were committed against more than one person during the same incident although only one of the victims was the subject of the sexual attack. There was just one case where the offending was perpetrated against a single victim over a prolonged period of time. The victim was living in the perpetrator's house, having moved in to clean and maintain the house for him as she had struggled financially since moving to Ireland. The sentencing judge stated that the defendant had treated the woman like a slave and sex object during this time. The prolonged period of offending was significant as was the abuse of a position of trust. Typically, offenders perpetrated these offence(s) alone although there were co-defendants in some instances.

The relationship between the parties

Sentences of this gravity were principally imposed where the perpetrator attacked a young woman that was either a stranger to them or a very recent acquaintance. Often described in sentencing remarks as a 'random attack' there was no clear rationale for targeting the specific person that was victimised as they were effectively not known to the perpetrator. This study identified 71 victims of sexual violence in these cases and almost two thirds of these victims were attacked by a stranger (64.8 per cent or 46 of 71, see Table 4.2). The next most prominent

Table 4.2: Relationship between victim and offender (adult victims)

Relationship to victim	Percentage	Number
Stranger	64.8%	46
Met within 24 hours of incident	18.3%	13
Acquaintance	8.5%	6
Partner or ex-partner	2.8%	2
Family relative	2.8%	2
Friend of the victim	1.4%	1
Employee	1.4%	1

Note: This does not include additional victims subject to non-sexual violence

relationship was where the victim and offender met within 24 hours of the incident (18.3 per cent or 13 of 71). These cases usually involved the offender meeting the victim at a pub, party or nightclub (11 of 13). The offender then isolated or tricked the victim in some manner and this then led to the sexual offending. In one case, the offender met the victim after she became separated from her friends on a hen night and lost her mobile phone. He brought her to a house under the pretence that she could make a phone-call but he raped, assaulted and falsely imprisoned her at the house. In cases where the parties were acquaintances but were known to each other for more than 24 hours, the nature of the 'acquaintance' relationship was tenuous. In two cases involving four victims the offender connected with the victims in advance of the offending *via* an 'escort' website. In another case, the defendant had met the victim previously in a pub where they agreed to go on a date. He committed the offences a week later. The relationships in the small number of remaining cases were diverse although the common theme was that the parties were known to each other in a more meaningful way.

The analysis identified a total of 60 different locations where the incidents took place.[12] Offending often occurred in a public place (such as a park, the countryside, a street, laneway, footpath or a vehicle in a public place) (40 per cent or 24 of 60). A further volume of incidents took place at either the home of the victim (26.7 per cent or 16 of 60) or the perpetrator (10 per cent or 6 of 60). The violation of the victim's dwelling or a home invasion is considered a significant aggravating factor.[13] There were also some incidents that occurred at a bed and breakfast or hotel accommodation (6.7 per cent or 4 of 60). The remaining cases (16.6 per cent or 10 of 60) occurred across a wide range of different locations including at a university department, a restaurant or place of employment.

Victims and their age

All of the victims of sexual violence were women and the majority were young adults. There were additional victims who were subject to non-sexual violence and many of these were men. In these cases, the man was assaulted or falsely imprisoned at the time of the perpetrator's sexual attack on the woman. The man was the partner of the woman at the time (six of seven). While this offending was of a serious nature in its own right, the intention of the perpetrator in attacking the man was to facilitate the sexual attack of the woman. In one additional case, the perpetrator abducted and abandoned the child of the woman he had attacked.

Where it was possible to identify the age of the victims of sexual violence, it was clear that these victims were young adults, with 40 per cent of victims aged between 18 to 24 and 23 per cent aged between 25 to 34. The youngest adult victim in cases resulting in a sentence of 15 years to life imprisonment was 20 at the time of victimisation. This victim was attacked at random by a stranger at night-time. This kind of fact pattern was replicated across many cases. In addition to the young adult age, the victims were often viewed as vulnerable by virtue of being alone at night in a public place. At the other end of the age spectrum, there were a number of instances (9 per cent) which involved offences committed against those over the age of 65. Elderly persons are vulnerable by virtue of their age and the victimisation of the elderly is an aggravating factor.[14] In a case where the offender entered the home of an 85-year-old woman and raped her repeatedly, the sentencing judge referenced the victim's age and vulnerability in assessing the gravity of the offending. In summary, the sentencing judge stated that 'this case is just about as bad as it gets'.[15] The remaining cases involved victims aged from 34 to 65 (28 per cent).

Alcohol and substance use

The evidence in these cases suggests that alcohol and substance use was a factor in offending although its impact on sentencing outcomes was complex. Offenders had consumed alcohol in 42.2 per cent of cases (19 of 45) prior to the commission of the offence(s). The commission of many of these offences occurred after the defendant and/or victim had been participants in the night-time economy. There were eight cases (17.7 per cent) where there was evidence that the perpetrator had consumed drugs or psychoactive substances. In all of these cases alcohol had also been consumed alongside these substances. The drugs consumed included cannabis, ecstasy, cocaine, methamphetamine and mephedrone. To illustrate, in one case a perpetrator had consumed 15 pints of beer and six shots as well as ecstasy and methamphetamine on a night out. After the consumption of these substances, he raped his girlfriend in the cubicle of a nightclub.

Taking alcohol and substance use into account as a factor in sentencing is complicated as it can be a mitigating, neutral or aggravating factor depending on the issue being considered within a specific case.[16] It may be viewed as an aggravating factor if the offender knew that the consumption of alcohol or drugs would have a negative impact on their behaviour. The courts have acknowledged that alcohol and substance use can be used in mitigation where it results in the defendant acting out of character or shows that the offence was not premeditated.[17] An assessment of these cases suggests that alcohol and substance use was viewed as either an aggravating or neutral factor. It was of particular concern when assessing the likelihood of reoffending. One judge noted, in a case where alcohol consumption was central to the offending, that unless the offender's substance use issues were addressed 'everyone from very young girls to very old ladies will be at risk'.[18]

Violence and culpability

All defendants are culpable for the offences that they have been convicted of, but at sentencing the judge must attempt to establish the degree of culpability and how this should be reflected in the sentence imposed. It is well established by the appellate courts that 'special violence, more than usual humiliation, or where the victim is subjected to additional and gratuitous sexual perversions' will have a serious impact on the sentence imposed.[19] The language of these aggravating factors is fairly general in nature and therefore it can be difficult to understand the level of violence that might elevate the offending into the most serious sentence category. Some understanding in terms of the level of violence, humiliation or perversion can be sourced in the descriptors employed by judges in assessing the offending. Words such as 'primal',[20] 'brutal',[21] 'outrageous',[22] 'savage'[23] and 'vicious'[24] are indicative of offending that was viewed as 'unique in falling to a new depth of depravity'.[25]

For the purposes of gaining greater insight into judicial assessments of the offending and the culpability of the offender, it is useful to examine some of the more specific elements of violence evident in cases resulting in a sentencing outcome of this severity. An important caveat to this is that individual cases are complex and the range of aggravating factors in a case can be very broad. No two sets of facts are the same and this analysis should be treated as simply providing a snapshot of some of the prevalent and identifiable aggravating factors of violence referenced in these cases rather than a full record of factors.

Implements of violence

The use of weapons, or the threat of their use, during the commission of these offences was a feature in 57.8 per cent of cases (26 of 45). Weapons were primarily used for the purpose of wielding authority but their use also arose as part of the perpetrator's sexual perversions in some cases. The use of a knife was the most common form of weapon but there were also instances where offenders used a baton, a towel handrail, a firearm or scissors. An offender convicted of the rape of two women entered their apartment on the premise that he had left money there. He then went into the kitchen and returned with a large knife which he used to threaten the women during three counts of rape, three counts of rape under s.4 and two counts of aggravated sexual assault. In a further case, the offender met the victim on a night out and offered to give her a lift. Instead he drove her to the mountains where he raped the victim a number of times. During this, he threatened her with a bottle of acid and a chainsaw. Causing, threatening or risking death or serious injury through the use of a weapon can also be categorised as special violence or humiliation so there is usually some overlap in terms of these aggravating factors. It is clear that the use or threat of the use of weapons contributed significantly to a sentence outcome of this length.

Death threats

The use of death threats was clearly a distinguishing factor in these cases. In over half of all cases, death threats were made to the victim either during the offending or afterwards (51.1 per cent or 23 of 45). Threats made during the offending were often part of an attempt to secure the submission of the victim(s) to sexual violence. In one case, the offender made 'credible' threats to the victim to 'slice her throat' if she made a noise during the offending, which lasted for 70 minutes.[26] Threats made subsequent to the offending related to pressuring the victim not to report the offending to the *Gardaí* or other people in their community. For instance, a perpetrator threatened to kill the victim's children if she reported the incident to the *Gardaí*. These threats were consistently viewed by judges as highly aggravating.

Tricking the victim

There were a number of cases (28.9 per cent or 13 of 45) where the victim was tricked in some manner rendering them more vulnerable to being attacked. For example, one perpetrator approached the victim, who was a sex worker, looking to pay for sex. After agreeing a price, he brought her down a laneway where he then assaulted and raped her. In another, the offender met the victim on a night out in Dublin and offered to give her a lift to another part of the city but instead drove her to the mountains where he raped her on a number of occasions. A further case shows how the defendant convinced a woman to go to an apartment on the pretence that there was an elderly woman there who was dying and was in need of help. Tricking a person into a position of vulnerability aligns with the pattern that many of these cases involved a random attack on an unsuspecting person engaged in ordinary and everyday activities.

Planning and premeditation

The planned and premeditated nature of an attack is an aggravating factor and it was specifically referenced by sentencing judges in a number of cases (15.6 per cent or 7 of 45). Although there was a high prevalence of attacks by strangers or by persons known to the victim within 24 hours of the offending, this does not mean that the attack was not planned or premeditated. Sentencing judges highlighted evidence that demonstrated that the offending was calculated. In a case where three victims were attacked by a stranger, the judge noted that the premeditated nature of the offending was evidenced by the fact that the perpetrator had packed zip ties, duct tape and a hunting knife in advance of the attacks. In a similar case involving the victimisation of two women who were strangers to the perpetrator, the judge noted that it was a 'highly aggravating factor … that the accused disclosed that he had planned the violation for some time and had been awaiting his opportunity'.[27] In a case involving an attack by the offender on his partner, the court described the offending as 'planned, predatory and premeditated'.[28] It is important to note that planning and premeditation should not be viewed as requiring a specific timeframe or level of detail. The planning can occur the day of the offending and up to or immediately beforehand. Its relevance in terms of the imposition of sentence goes to the assessment of the level of culpability of the offender.

The harm caused to the victim(s)

The harm caused to the victim is a key component in assessing the gravity of the offence. As O'Malley notes, 'consequences that were reasonably foreseeable and that actually occurred may be taken into account when assessing harm'.[29] This may include the physical, emotional, mental or economic effects in the immediate aftermath of the offending, up to and including the medium- and long-term consequences of the victimisation. Brown synthesises the non-physical harms experienced by victims of sexual violence documented in the research as including: 'shame and humiliation; altered relationships with others; reputational damage; loss of employment prospects; victim blaming; withdrawal from social life; anxiety, paranoia, depression and low self-esteem'.[30] Unsurprisingly, references to the harm caused to the victim were explicitly identifiable in almost all cases (93.3 per cent or 42 of 45). In summarising the harm caused, the language reflected the severity of consequences resulting from the defendant's actions. Judges referred to the 'catastrophic effect' of the offending resulting in lives being 'permanently disrupted'.[31]

The physical, emotional and psychological impact of the offending was frequently referenced when articulating the harm caused during the offending and the long-term impact of this for the victim(s). A sentencing judge noted that in a case where the victim was attacked by a stranger, a consequence of the offending was that the life of the victim had been 'rendered into a changed state'.[32] An attack on an elderly woman was described by the judge as a 'life-changing experience'.[33] There were some cases where the judge noted the severe, long-term and irreversible consequences of the physical harm caused. In one case, the victim was left with a serious brain injury as a result of the assault where, as the judge noted, the victim's 'room for improvement is modest'.[34]

Victim impact statements were particularly instructive in informing judges of the range of harms caused. Introduced by legislation in 1993, victim impact statements have become an important part of a sentencing hearing.[35] A court may receive evidence or submissions from the victim at sentencing on the impact of the offending on the victim. The evidence included in the statement may relate to the physical, mental, emotional and economic harm caused by the offending.[36] The court is required to take account of the effect of the offending on the victim.[37]

Victim impact statements were specifically referenced by judges in 62.2 per cent of cases (28 of 45).[38] In assessing the harm to the victim, judges referred to the statements provided by victims as 'quite visceral'[39] and 'chilling'.[40] In a case involving the rape of two women, the judge noted 'that very great harm was caused as a result of the offending in each case as is obvious from the eloquent and lengthy impact statements'.[41] Victim impact statements were viewed as particularly useful in informing the judge of the medium- and long-term impact of the offending on the victim. One judge noted that '[r]eading the statements of the six individual victims would almost render one speechless at the indignity, horror, and terror they have been subjected to'.[42] Another described how the offending 'permanently disrupted and, in fact, ruined both women's lives'.[43] Victim impact statements also detailed the impact the offending had on the victim's relationships. One victim described how the offending led to the breakdown of her 23-year relationship and that it also had a negative impact on her relationship with her children and grand-children.

There has been an ongoing debate among criminal justice scholars regarding what role, if any, victim impact statements should play in influencing sentencing outcomes. The core of the debate relates to whether these statements are compatible with the proportionality principle.[44] Opponents argue that victim impact statements may impair the objectivity of the process or shift focus from legitimate sentencing factors, risking a disproportionate outcome. Engaging in this debate is beyond the scope of this book but it is clear that judges have a high regard for victim input. Informing the judge of the impact and consequences for the victim, their lives and the lives of those around them, was viewed as instructive and valuable information in assessing the harm caused.

Assessing the offender

All of the perpetrators in cases resulting in these sentencing outcomes were men. At the time of offending, the age of the perpetrators ranged from 15 to 65 (see Table 4.3). Many defendants were at a relatively young age when committing these offences. There were co-defendants in three cases and these related to sexual offences that were characterised as a 'gang rape'. A gang rape is considered a seriously aggravating factor as it is 'a terrifying experience for the victim' and increases the likelihood of serious harm.[45] Outside of an assessment of the gravity of the offence and the harm caused

Table 4.3: Age of offender at time of offending (adult victims)

Age	Percentage	Number
Under 18	2.2%	1
18–24	22.2%	10
25–34	35.6%	16
35–44	26.7%	12
45–54	11.1%	5
55+	2.2%	1

to the victim, judges also appeared to be influenced by factors pertaining more directly to the offender. The most significant factor of influence was where an offender had convictions prior to the offences that they were currently being sentenced for. This was sometimes connected, alongside other available information, to the risk of reoffending.

Previous criminal history

Previous criminal history is an important factor in sentencing in many jurisdictions,[46] as well as a factor in assessing the risk of reoffending.[47] In terms of Irish sentencing practice, there was a lack of clarity as to whether it could be incorporated as an aggravating factor in sentencing up until 2008. The position was clarified in an appellate decision where a sentence of life imprisonment for aggravated sexual assault was being challenged in the Court of Criminal Appeal. The court held that previous convictions are relevant 'in aggravation of the offence' and 'form part of the matrix of circumstances to which the court should have regard in determining an appropriate sentence'.[48] This is the case for 'like offences' or offences that are similar to the offence(s) for which the person is currently being sentenced (for example, a previous conviction for rape is relevant in a sentencing hearing for a current rape offence).[49] Repeat offending in sexual offences was addressed by legislation in 2019. If a person convicted of a sexual offence resulting in a period of imprisonment of 5 years (or more) is subsequently convicted (within 10 years) of a sexual offence with a maximum term of life imprisonment, the judge must specify a minimum term of 10 years when imposing a sentence.[50]

Offenders being sentenced had a previous criminal history in two thirds of these cases (66.7 per cent or 30 of 45). There was no previous criminal history in 24.4 per cent of cases (11 of 45).[51] Out of the cases where previous convictions were identifiable, 60 per cent (18 of 30) involved sexual offences and these were often of a serious nature. In eight of these cases the offender had previously been convicted of rape (including the victimisation of adults and children). There were also cases where the offences were at the medium-to-lower level in terms of penalty severity, such as sexual assaults and indecency offences. Judges described prior convictions for sexual offences as 'deeply worrying'[52] and 'an overwhelmingly serious matter'.[53] Aside from sexual offences, previous criminal history included a range of offending, from the most serious crimes (including three offenders with previous convictions for murder or manslaughter) to convictions at the lower level (including road traffic or public order offences). Burglary, theft, false imprisonment and assaults were the non-sexual offences that appeared most frequently in these offenders' previous criminal history. In addition to previous convictions, there were a couple of cases where the defendant committed serious sexual offences while on bail for another offence and, since 1997, this must be treated as an aggravating factor.[54]

The risk of reoffending

Public protection and the risk of reoffending was referenced by sentencing judges in 51.1 per cent of cases (23 of 45). It was possible to identify specific references to risk assessment tools or evidence from experts in a number of cases. Since 2005, judges have access to a risk assessment report conducted by the Probation Service.[55] This information was valuable in formulating a determination on the issue of public protection. One judge, referencing information in a psychological assessment and Probation Service report, described the offender as a 'most dangerous person'.[56]

There were many instances where judges used the language of risk and dangerousness in their sentencing remarks, describing the offender as: a 'menace';[57] 'a grave threat';[58] and a 'danger to society'.[59] In explaining a 15-year sentence for the rape of an elderly woman by an offender with previous convictions for rape and false imprisonment, the trial judge noted that the offender 'needs to be removed from society until it's safe for him to return'.[60] This type of sentiment was echoed by many judges with a clear concern in relation to the risk posed to the public and, more specifically, women. The level of violence, the number of victims, the random nature of the attack and, in particular, a previous criminal history all contributed to judges concluding that the offender posed a risk to the public. Where the risk of reoffending was referenced in sentencing remarks, two thirds of defendants also had a previous criminal history (15 of 23).

Judges are in an especially difficult position in cases where an offender is young but there is a perception that they are at a risk of reoffending on release. A child or young adult may have their age taken into account in mitigation.[61] A difficulty arises in cases where the evidence may indicate that the young defendant is at a high risk of reoffending and a reduced sentence could mean that they will be still be relatively young on release. The situation is best illustrated with an example. In a case where the defendant was 18 at the time of the commission of the offences, the judge noted that he considered a sentence of life imprisonment but imposed a 15-year sentence in light of the defendant's age. Taking remission of 25 per cent into consideration, this offender could conceivably be released after 11.25 years in custody and would still be a young man. Concerned about risk on release, the judge also imposed a ten-year post release supervision order in addition to the 15-year sentence 'to keep him under control'.[62] In the context of cases where there is a perception that the offender poses a significant risk of reoffending, age can be a difficult matter for a court to address.

Assessing mitigating factors

To impose a proportionate sentence, the judge must take into consideration any mitigating factors arising. It was possible to identify mitigating factors in 60 per cent of cases (27 of 45) but it was sometimes unclear as to how much of a reduction, if any, was being applied as the headline sentence was not identifiable in many cases. That being said, a numerical value for mitigation was sourced in 13 cases and the value ranged from one to nine years, with most cases (11) falling within one to five years. In Ireland, the range of potential mitigating factors is extensive. In the cases in this study, it was evident that the defendant's response to charges made the most significant contribution to mitigation. Offence-related and personal mitigation were far less prevalent in sentencing remarks.

Response to charges includes a guilty plea and/or cooperation with the investigation. In over half of all cases, the defendant pleaded guilty to all charges (55.5 per cent or 25 of 45).[63] In addition, the defendant's cooperation with the investigation was also referenced by judges as contributing to the calculation of mitigation. The stage at which a defendant enters a guilty plea is of great importance in terms of the level of discount applied to the sentence. The plea was most frequently entered at the first reasonable opportunity (44 per cent or 11 of 25). In the remainder, the plea was entered post charge but before the trial (28 per cent or 7 of 25) or during the trial (12 per cent or 3 of 25).[64] A guilty plea entered early in the process should ordinarily attract a significant discount (approximately 15 to 30 per cent).[65] However, the later the plea, the less likely a reduction will be applied. Pleading guilty during the course of a trial, for example, is of little value, especially when the defendant is 'caught red-handed'.[66] A late plea for sexual offences is a critical issue as it will result in the victim being subjected to the distress of the trial process. The level of reduction may also be impacted where the defendant pleaded guilty early in the process but there is no realistic evidential basis to contest guilt.

The guilty plea discount varied depending on the case and was sometimes described as partial rather than full. A discount of four years was applied in a case where the defendant entered a guilty plea at a 'relatively early stage' for two sexual attacks on two women on separate occasions.[67] The judge stated that the headline sentence pre-mitigation was 20 years. At the other end of the spectrum, there were cases where a guilty plea resulted in either a minimal discount or no discount at all. A one-year discount was applied in a case where a defendant pleaded guilty to rape, kidnapping and attempted murder, with the judge acknowledging that although the offending was 'truly horrific' the plea had freed time in court to 'deal with some other violent person'.[68] There were a number of cases where a reduction in sentence was not applied despite the entering of a guilty plea and this was either due to the lateness of the plea or the exceptional nature of the offending (for a discussion on the guilty plea discount in exceptional cases see Chapter 6).

Alongside a guilty plea and cooperation with the investigation, expressions of remorse were identified in relation to mitigation in 15.5 per cent of cases (seven of 45). It is up to the judge to assess the credibility of the expressions of remorse to determine whether it is genuine and warrants a reduction.[69] In a case where the defendant had written a letter detailing his remorse, the judge noted that while the law required to give him the benefit of the doubt, he had serious reservations as to the genuineness of the remorse. The opposite was the case where a trial judge noted that the headline sentence was life imprisonment but that the guilty plea and the genuine remorse warranted a reduction to 18 years' imprisonment. Ultimately, this is a matter for judges to decide based on information that may support or undermine the assertion of remorse.

As already discussed, a young person may be afforded mitigation by virtue of their age. An elderly offender or those with age-related health issues may also benefit from mitigation. A sentence was reduced from life imprisonment to 15 years in part due to considerations as to the age (68) and health of the defendant. There were a number of cases where personal mitigation in the form of physical and mental health issues and/or intellectual disabilities were raised, although not always successfully. There was little evidence that an offender's 'dysfunctional' background or substance use issues were taken into account, although these may be factors considered by a judge.[70] An offender's conduct in custody and willingness to engage in rehabilitative services did arise as a factor in the mitigation of a sentence in some cases. Given the severity of the offending, offence-related mitigation was rarely referenced. Mitigating factors such as a defendant taking steps to alleviate the effects of the offence or a defendant not intending to cause serious injury, would be inconsistent with prior assessments of gravity and culpability.

In some cases judges explicitly stated that there were no mitigating factors of substance arising and therefore a reduction was not considered appropriate (17.8 per cent or 8 of 45).[71] In a case where an offender raped an elderly woman, the trial judge stated, in sentencing the defendant to 21 years, that there were no mitigating factors and noted that the offender had already been afforded leniency in sentencing for a previous conviction for the rape of a child (12 years' imprisonment). The judge stated that the offender had 'spurned' that leniency by raping another person on release.[72] In a case where the defendant was sentenced to 15 years for rape, the judge remarked that there was 'nothing significant in favour of the accused to allow any discount'.[73] Given the rarity of sentences being imposed at this level of severity, it comes as no surprise that mitigation in these cases would either be limited, partial or non-existent.

Selecting life imprisonment

It is important to try to understand what influences a sentencing judge to impose the ultimate penalty of life imprisonment and this was detailed to some extent in Chapter 3. Looking more specifically at this cohort of cases, there were ten instances where life imprisonment was imposed and the analysis demonstrates that rather than these cases being materially different to those resulting in determinate sentences, there may simply be a higher rate or combination of aggravating factors prevalent in cases of life imprisonment. Almost all offenders were convicted of multiple offences (nine of ten). In terms of the gravity of the offending, there was a higher rate of the use of death threats (eight of ten), the use or the threat of the use of implements of violence (seven of ten) than established in the general analysis just discussed. In addition, almost all of those that were subject to life imprisonment had a previous criminal history (nine of ten) and these included convictions for sexual offences (eight of ten). In terms of mitigating factors, defendants did plead guilty at a similar rate to those in receipt of determinate sentences (six of ten) but this plea was either late or did not result in a reduction due to the exceptional nature of the offending. It is possible that a higher level of violence (and harm) as well as a significant previous criminal history including sexual offences may have been central to the assessment that life imprisonment was warranted in these cases. At the same time, many cases resulting in a life sentence were almost indistinguishable from their determinate counterparts and the rationale for imposing a life sentence over a determinate sentence was not easily ascertained when examining the gravity of the offence.

Sentencing and the 'real rape' myth

'Rape myths' refer to stereotypical and often damaging attitudes about the commission of the offence and those most likely to be a perpetrator or victim of this crime.[74] The 'real rape' myth encapsulates the misperception that rape often involves a sudden, surprise attack by a stranger in a public place using force and/or weapons resulting in physical injury.[75] The 'ideal victim' refers to a status conferred on some victims that are fully and completely viewed by the public and the criminal justice system as legitimate by virtue of specific traits that they hold and in rape cases, it is often young, female victims who are perceived as weak, virtuous, respectable and beyond reproach.[76] Rape and victimhood is much more diverse and complex than these stereotypes allow. Cases and victims that do not fit easily with these characteristics and traits are less likely to be viewed by the public and criminal justice decision-makers as genuine. Research indicates that this can impact whether cases are investigated by the police, prosecuted or result in a conviction by a jury.[77] Less time has been spent looking at the impact of 'rape myths' on sentencing decision-makers but, given the profile of cases resulting in the most severe sentences detailed in this chapter, it is worth taking some time to consider whether 'rape myths' operate as an influencing factor on sentencing judge's perceptions of seriousness.

There are some clear connections with the 'real rape' narrative and the factors evident in the analysis of cases resulting in 15 years to life imprisonment. The offending was perpetrated by a stranger in a public place, resulted in physical injury and involved the use of weapons and/or threats. Victims were young women and often described by judges as 'vulnerable'. Of course, evidence of the use of weapons, death threats and physical injury are not just part of the 'real rape' narrative, they are also aggravating factors that judges are required to take into consideration in sentencing. So too is the age of the victim – the young and the elderly are legally viewed as more vulnerable and attacking either is an aggravating factor. More difficult to understand is the prevalence of 'stranger' rapes in cases resulting in 15 years to life imprisonment.

In this study, 64.8 per cent of victims were attacked by a stranger and 18.3 per cent by a person they met within 24 hours. This is in contrast with data on the experience of sexual violence in Ireland which indicates that the majority of adult victims knew the person who perpetrated the violence (78 per cent) and this person was often a partner, former partner, friend or acquaintance.[78] Studies conducted in other jurisdictions also show that most serious sexual offences (such as rape) are perpetrated by those known to the victim.[79] Information on the relationship between perpetrator and victim arising in serious sexual offences is somewhat limited in Ireland, although a number of studies have found that the majority of rapes were perpetrated by a person known to the victim.[80] An analysis of rape trials in the Central Criminal Court demonstrated that the parties had a prior relationship of some description in almost three quarters of cases.[81] In 26.4 per cent of cases the defendant had no personal relationship to the victim.

A detailed analysis of sentencing patterns in sexual offence or rape cases is not possible due to a lack of data in Ireland. As a result, it is not clear whether the prevalence of stranger relationships in cases at the top end of the penalty range is an anomaly, incidental to these decisions, or a contributing factor to judicial deliberations. Nonetheless, there is a valid concern that the prevalence of this pattern of cases inadvertently embeds 'real rape' myths in guidance judgments, which are drawn from these sentencing decisions. The appellate court's reliance on these decisions in creating and articulating guidance for sentences of 15 years to life imprisonment may then have an impact on sentencing judges' deliberations in future cases. Of course, it may simply be that these are the types of cases appearing before the courts for sentencing on a more frequent basis. A recent survey found that those who experienced sexual violence as an adult with a non-partner were three times more likely to disclose this to someone than those who experienced sexual violence with a partner.[82] This in itself presents a major challenge as many relationship-based sexual violence cases are not reaching the criminal justice system despite being more prevalent in society generally. It is also possible that when deliberating on sentence outcomes, judges perceive stranger rape as being more serious and harmful. These issues are not unique to Ireland. International research shows that sentencing judges demonstrate a reluctance to impose adequate sentences in cases of sexual violence perpetrated by a partner or ex-partner.[83] As the number of cases in this study is small and rich data on general sentencing patterns in sexual offences is lacking, it is difficult to draw any definitive conclusions here. Further research is needed in this area.

A counterargument to the idea that the relationship between the parties is a factor of significance might be that it is the levels of violence, physical injury and harm caused that results in the selection of a sentence of this severity. However, the stereotype that 'stranger' rapes are more violent than rapes in other relationship contexts is not necessarily supported by some of the international research.[84] A number of studies have found that physical violence and injury is actually more common in cases where the victim had been sexually assaulted by a partner than by a stranger.[85] In addition, intimate partner sexual violence also involves a breach of trust and this is a long-established aggravating factor in sentencing. In fact, recent legislation has specified that where an offence is committed by a spouse, partner or intimate partner (current or former), the relationship is to be treated as an aggravating factor in sentencing for the offences of rape, rape under s.4 and aggravated sexual assault.[86]

Associating stranger relationship sexual violence with being more harmful or more serious than sexual violence perpetrated in other relationships is problematic. The concern is that judges may be exercising their discretion to elevate offending perpetrated by strangers into the most serious penalty range to the exclusion of other offending that may be similarly violent, culpable and harmful but perpetrated by a person known to the victim. In England and Wales, appellate decisions and sentencing guidelines state that judges should adopt the same starting point for the sentence irrespective of the relationship.[87] Irish policy-makers and judicial decision-makers should reflect on how to effectively address relationship and non-relationship sexual violence in a way that does not succumb to the stereotypes of the 'real rape' myth.

Conclusion

The analysis of factors in these cases revealed a very specific fact pattern. The cases involved serious levels of violence including death threats and the use of weapons, the resultant impact of which was a high degree of harm to the victim(s). This included physical, psychological and emotional harms that impacted victims in the short, medium and long term. Additionally, the previous criminal history of the offender and the perception that there was a risk of reoffending is relevant in understanding the sentence outcome in these cases. A factor of major importance was the number of offences for which the offender was being sentenced. While judges were often sentencing the offender for a single incident, the offender had committed multiple offences during the course of this incident. The prominence of 'stranger' rapes committed against young women in public places indicates that sentencing judges may view this type of offending as being the most serious violation worthy of the most severe penalty. The connection between these cases and the 'real rape' myth raises questions as to whether perceptions based on the relationship between the parties are impacting sentence severity. Certainly, the relationship between the parties is only one part of the picture in terms of assessing the offending but it does demonstrate the importance of taking a broad and holistic view of sentencing decision-making. In the next chapter, which deals with sentencing cases of child sexual abuse, judges were sentencing offenders for a multiplicity of offences over a prolonged period of time and these offences were usually committed by a family member. A very different profile and set of factors emerged in the analysis.

FIVE

Sentencing crimes of child sexual abuse

Introduction

In cases of child sexual abuse where a sentence of 15 years to life imprisonment was imposed, the offender was often a family member of the victim. Children were victimised at a young age and were repeatedly victimised over a prolonged period of time. The abuse of a position of trust or authority contributed to elevating this offending into the most serious sentencing band. Offenders were not only convicted of multiple offences, there was a significant volume of cases where judges were imposing sentences for the victimisation of multiple children. The sheer quantity of offences committed was, at times, staggering.

Aggravating factors similar to adult victims that related to the use of special violence, threats and coercion were also present. A parallel between adult and child victims was the level of harm caused to the victim by the offending although the types of harm caused varied. References to the defendant's previous criminal history were less prevalent in sentencing remarks when compared with cases involving adult victims. But this should be situated in the context of offending that often persisted for long periods against multiple victims and may not have been disclosed by the victim until many years into adulthood. Mitigating factors were few and far between. Even where there was an early admission of guilt the reduction in sentence was often limited. This chapter examines 63 cases where sentences of 15 years to life imprisonment have been imposed by judges from 1985 to 2022 for offences committed against child victims. The key factors influencing the decision to impose a sentence of this length is given detailed analysis and consideration. The chapter concludes with a discussion of how social and legal evolutions on child sexual abuse in Ireland helped shape these cases coming before the courts.

The offences and sentences

Defendants accused of committing a sexual offence where the victim is a child may be charged and convicted of an offence specific to the victimisation of children, such as the offence of defilement of a child under the age of 15.[1] Key to this offence is that the child, by virtue of their age, does not have the capacity to consent to a sexual act. Consent is no defence. A sexual act includes sexual intercourse, aggravated sexual assault and rape under s.4. Defilement of a child under the age of 15 carries a maximum penalty of life imprisonment.[2] Defendants may also be convicted of the range of sexual offences that are not limited by age, including rape, rape under s.4 and aggravated sexual assault. These offences also have a maximum penalty of life imprisonment. If a person is accused of the rape of a 14-year-old they may be prosecuted for the offence of rape or the offence of defilement of a child under the age of 15. The facts may fit within the definition of both offences. It is up to the prosecution to make the decision as to how to classify the offending; however the defendant cannot be convicted of both offences for a single act.

The principal offence in these cases was the offence of rape or rape under s.4 (95.2 per cent or 60 of 63). In just 3.2 per cent of cases (two of 63) the defendant was convicted of a defilement of a child offence. One remaining case (1.6 per cent) involved a defendant sentenced to consecutive sentences for 'indecent assault' against young boys in the 1950s and 1960s. Many of these offences, which were reported to the authorities decades later, would likely be prosecuted as rape under s.4 using existing law and practice today. It is important to note that judges were sentencing offenders for multiple sexual offences in each case. In many instances there were offences committed that were viewed as equal in terms of offence seriousness and, as a result, the use of the term 'principal offence' may be somewhat misleading (see The multiplicity of offending).

Similar to cases involving adult victims, there was a propensity to impose a sentence at the lowest and highest end of the sentence range in this study. In almost half of all cases (47.6 per cent or 30 of 63) the sentence imposed was 15 years' imprisonment. Judges imposed life imprisonment in one in every five cases (19.1 per cent or 12 of 63). In between these two ends of the spectrum, most sentences imposed were greater than 15 years and up to (and including) 20 years (30.1 per cent or 19 of 63) with only two determinate sentences exceeding 20 years imprisonment (3.2 per cent or two of 63). Sentences were almost always imposed concurrently (88.9 per cent or 56 of 63), rather than consecutively (11.1 per cent or 7 of 63). The cases where consecutive sentences were imposed involved multiple incidents and more than half involved multiple victims (four of seven). They often included concurrent sentences imposed alongside consecutive sentences. In just under two thirds of determinate sentence cases (60.7 per cent or 31 of 51) the sentencing judge suspended a part of the sentence and this period of suspension ranged from one to seven years. Since 2001, a post-release supervision order was identified in 39 per cent (16 of 41) of determinate sentence cases and this was often as a result of concern in relation to the risk of reoffending (see Assessing the offender). There were four instances where there were co-accused.

Long-term imprisonment was more frequently imposed by judges in recent years. Fifteen years to life was imposed in only one quarter of cases (15 of 63) in the first half of the study (1985 to 2003). The remaining three quarters of cases (48 of 63) were in the latter half (2004 to 2022). The delay in disclosure in many of these cases is a significant factor here. For example, there were instances of sentences being imposed for non-recent child sexual abuse that pre-dated this study in the 1970s and early 1980s. There have been tangible legal and societal shifts that may also have impacted disclosures and prosecutions of child sexual abuse (see Delay and the evolving responses to child sexual abuse). There are many other additional factors that are beyond the scope of this book that may help explain changing patterns in cases coming before the courts.

The gravity of the offence

In terms of assessing the gravity of the offence, sentencing judges expressed clearly that the offending was at 'the very apex of seriousness' and in the top range of the penalty.[3] Judges described the offending in language reflecting the extremity of the violence and violation, calling it 'depraved',[4] 'horrific'[5] and of the 'utmost gravity'.[6] Acknowledging the limitations of sentencing in addressing the gravity of the offending, one judge remarked that '[w]hatever sentence I give is an inadequate reflection of the horrors of the abuse'.[7] The level of seriousness was so pronounced that sentencing judges described the offending as 'abhorrent'[8] and 'evil',[9] resulting in the victims' lives being 'a permanent execution'.[10] To gain a greater understanding of the offending beyond this emotive language, it is useful to explore some of the key factors that elevated the offending into the most serious category for sentencing judges. The factors identified by the Supreme Court for the most serious sentencing band of 15 years to life imprisonment are evident in these cases (see Table 2.1, Chapter 2). The levels of violence, the harm caused to the victim and the relationship between the parties were all of great importance. It should be noted that the analysis cannot provide an account of all factors and is best understood as a representation of those most frequently identified factors based on the available materials.

The multiplicity of offending

Judges identified the 'length, intensity and depravity of the sexual abuse'[11] and the 'multiplicity of the offences'[12] as a central factor in sentence selection. The Supreme Court have stated that a series of offences is an aggravating factor that may warrant a headline sentence of 15 years to life imprisonment.[13] In every single case, multiple offences were committed and these all included additional sexual offences.

The number of sexual offences the defendant was convicted of ranged from two to 227. In two thirds of these cases, the offender was convicted of between two and 19 sexual offences (see Table 5.1). There were five cases where the offender had been convicted of over 100 sexual offences. In some cases, the volume of offending being dealt with at sentencing is an underrepresentation of the original charges. In almost half of the cases (46 per cent or 29 of 63) the offender had been convicted of only a sample of the charges on the indictment. A man charged with 264 offences for the rape and sexual abuse of two young children was convicted of 23 sample charges

Table 5.1: Total number of sexual offences at sentencing (child victims)

Offence range	Number of cases	Percentage of cases
1 to 9	23	36.5%
10 to 19	19	30.2%
20 to 29	6	9.5%
30 to 39	3	4.8%
40 to 49	1	1.6%
50 plus	11	17.4%

Table 5.2: Incidents and victims in sexual offence cases (child victims)

	Single victim	Multiple victims
Single incident	0 0.0%	2 3.2%
Multiple incidents	27 42.9%	34 53.9%

Table 5.3: Duration of victimisation per case (child victims)

Time period	Number	Percentage
Up to 24 hours	5	8.9%
1 day < 1 year	4	7.2%
1 year < 5 years	12	21.4%
5 years < 10 years	14	25.0%
10 years < 15 years	13	23.2%
15 years < 20 years	5	8.9%
20 years < 25 years	3	5.4%

Note: Excludes seven cases where significant gaps in offending were identified

following the entering of a guilty plea. He was sentenced to 18 years' imprisonment with three years suspended. A further aggravating factor in these cases is that over half of the cases involved offences committed against multiple children (see Table 5.2).

In terms of the prolonged nature of the offending, cases ranged from a single incident perpetrated against multiple victims to offending that persisted against victims over a 23-year period (see Table 5.3). The length of victimisation was not easy to calculate. In some cases, there were significant gaps between different incidents perpetrated against different victims. For example, in one case a defendant was being sentenced for sexual offences that occurred between 1987–1990 and 1997–2005. Excluding cases where there were significant time gaps (seven), half of the cases involved offending that persisted from five to 15 years. What is evident from the data is that a key driver of these sentence outcomes was the volume, breadth and persistent nature of the offending.

Young and vulnerable victims

The abuse of young and vulnerable victims is a serious aggravating factor as is the victimisation of multiple children.[14] Offending that targets young children was viewed as highly exploitative of the 'weak and defenceless'.[15] A total of 159 child victims of sexual violence were identified across 63 cases. There were multiple victims in more than half of the cases (57.1 per cent or 36 of 63) and the number of victims in each case ranged from two to ten. In the majority of cases involving multiple victims, judges imposed concurrent sentences for all offences (88.9 per cent or 32 of 36). There were four cases where consecutive sentences were imposed (11.1 per cent or four of 36) and these cases all involved three or more victims. In three of these four cases the relationship between the perpetrator and the victim was extrafamilial. The high volume of offending in these cases, the number of victims, the pursuit of sample charges and the tendency to impose concurrent rather than consecutive sentences means that defendants are in receipt of a significantly reduced sentence by virtue of all the offending being dealt with at the same hearing.

In addition to the aggravating factor of offences being perpetrated against multiple victims, the young age of the victim(s) is important in terms of assessing both the culpability of the offender and of the harm caused to the victim(s).[16] The appellate courts have stated that the victimisation of a young child is especially aggravating as sexual abuse has a seriously adverse impact on the development of a child through to adolescence and into adulthood.[17] As offending often continued for an extended period of time, judges frequently provided an age range, documenting the age at which the offending began and ended. But in cases where there were multiple victims, it was not always possible to identify the age range for each individual victim. As a result, it is challenging to present complete information on the issue of age, but some data can be extracted that may be valuable. The youngest victim across these cases was 1.5 years of age when the offending commenced. In fact, there were ten cases (15.9 per cent) where the offender began victimising a child or children before the age of five. In a further 34 cases (54.0 per cent), the child or children were aged from five to ten years when the offending commenced.

The picture in terms of gender is more diverse here than in adult cases, with almost a third of victims being male (50 of 159). In most cases the victims were either female (71.4 per cent or 45 of 63) or male (15.8 per cent or 10 of 63), but there were some cases where the offender victimised both male and female children (11.1 per cent or 7 of 63). The overall higher ratio of female victims in this band of sentencing is evidence of the gendered nature of child sexual abuse. A global meta-analysis on the pervasiveness of child sexual abuse demonstrated a prevalence rate of 13 per cent among a sample of 10 million individuals.[18] The research found that girls were twice as likely as boys to be victims of child sexual abuse. The site of offending against child victims was in a private location (92.1 per cent or 58 of 63), often the home of both the victim and offender.

Abusing a position of trust

The abuse of a position of trust and the misuse of a dominant position within a family are long-established aggravating factors in sexual offence cases and, factually, these factors arose in cases of child sexual abuse resulting in long-term imprisonment.[19] Intrafamilial relationships emerged as the central relationship between the parties, with 60.4 per cent of victims being abused by a family member (see Table 5.4). The most prominent relationship was that of father or step-father to the victim.[20] Indeed, research indicates that where sexual abuse is

Table 5.4: Relationship between victim and offender (child victims)

Relationship to victim	Percentage	Number
Father	36.5%	58
Step-father	8.8%	14
Uncle	6.9%	11
Brother	0.6%	1
Other family relative	7.6%	12
Friend of the family	8.2%	13
Neighbour	2.5%	4
Acquaintance	10.7%	17
Stranger	3.2%	5
Employee of parents of victim	4.4%	7
School teacher	3.7%	6
Priest	1.9%	3
Other/unidentified	5.0%	8

intrafamilial, the majority of those convicted of these offences are fathers or step-fathers.[21] Outside of family members, a significant number of offenders had some form of a relationship with either the victim or their family, such as a neighbour or friend of the family. Effectively, there was some level of trust that existed between the offender and the victim(s), and/or their family members.

There were also cases where the offender abused their position of authority and trust, for example as a school teacher or a priest. In a case where the offender was the victim's teacher, the judge gave little weight to mitigating factors, stating: 'To weigh up all the matters to the credit of the accused is to undermine the appalling breach by him of the trust imposed on him as a teacher and relied upon by six innocent children'.[22] In a further case where the defendant was a priest, the sentencing judge stated that it was difficult to imagine a more reprehensible circumstance 'than a priest in confession setting about the sexual abuse of a boy'.[23] In contrast to cases involving adult victims, only a very small number of offenders were strangers to the victim (3.2 per cent or 5 of 159). There were notable differences when examining the relationships between the parties using gender as a lens. Four out of five female victims were victimised by a family member (89 of 109) whereas three out of every five male victims (36 of 50) were victimised by non-family members. The reasons for this are not entirely clear although it is important to emphasise that these findings only relate to the decisions of judges to impose a sentence of long-term imprisonment in what they view as the most serious level of offending. A recent survey did find that women who experienced sexual violence as a child were more likely to have experienced this with a family member/relative (23 per cent) when compared with men who experienced sexual violence as a child (16 per cent).[24] Conversely, men were more likely to have experienced sexual violence as a child from a person in authority (13 per cent) when compared with women (5 per cent).

Grooming or tricking the victim(s)

In addition to the breach of trust and misuse of a dominant position arising from the relationship between the parties, evidence that the defendant groomed, manipulated or tricked the victim further increases the culpability of the offender.[25] Given the prolonged nature of offending in these cases, it was apparent that some offenders 'dominated and controlled' their victims for many years.[26] In a sentencing handbook prepared by the Judicial Researchers' Office, it is noted that 'systematic grooming' and 'plying a victim with alcohol' are aggravating factors in sexual offence cases.[27] In some instances alcohol, drugs or cigarettes were used to groom young victims.[28] One judge noted that the defendant would ply the victim with substantial amounts of alcohol resulting in her suffering liver damage. Evidence that a perpetrator engaged in a 'pattern of control' of the victim(s) or was 'methodically' grooming children was regarded as highly aggravating.[29]

Special violence, death threats and implements of violence

There are a number of aggravating factors that relate to the level and extent of violence perpetrated against the victim(s) including: special violence and more than usual humiliation; additional and gratuitous sexual perversions; the use of death threats; and the use of implements of violence for the purpose of wielding authority or sexual perversion.[30] There was evidence of these factors individually or combined in a number of cases. There were six instances (9.5 per cent) where there was evidence that the offender used death threats during or after the offending. In one case, the offender had threatened the three victims (who were sisters) to such a degree that each girl was unaware that her siblings were being abused. There were instances of extreme violence, degradation and the use of weapons. A defendant was sentenced to 15 years for offences perpetrated against his child and wife. In addition to being convicted of multiple counts of rape of his daughter, the defendant had chained both victims to a wall and violently assaulted them using weapons including razor blades, a screwdriver and a saw blade. There were 11 cases (17.5 per cent) where the defendant had used, or threatened to use, implements of violence. These threats occurred during the offending, or afterwards, often in an attempt to secure the silence of the victim(s). There were also instances where implements of violence and threats were used together, for example through threatening a victim at knife point.

During the analysis of these cases, it was apparent that the facts of the offending itself were not as detailed as cases where adults were the victims of sexual violence. It is possible that this may be attributed to the sheer volume of offending that needed to be communicated in the sentencing remarks. Cases involving adult victims arose from a single incident and more details as to the facts of that specific incident were provided. Judges also expressed difficulties in detailing the facts in cases of child sexual abuse given the extremity and depravity of the violence involved (for a discussion see Chapter 6). The threshold in relation to special violence, gratuitous sexual perversions and humiliation is established by virtue of the volume of offending, the age and vulnerability of the victim(s) and the relationship between the parties. As one judge surmised, these are cases of 'unparalleled cruelty'.[31]

Recording and dissemination of sexual violence

In 2021, the Court of Appeal established that the recording and/or dissemination of a recording is evidence of increased culpability and harm to the victim in sexual offence cases.[32] Image-based or technology-facilitated sexual violence subjects the victim(s) to an additional level of violation and harm.[33] The Court of Appeal acknowledged that there were already cases where judges had treated recording and/or dissemination as an aggravating factor. Since the 2000s in particular, recording of the crime(s) was evident in a small number of cases. The Court of Appeal, when increasing a sentence from 15 years to life imprisonment noted, in addition to evidence of serious sexual abuse, the father had taken inappropriate photographs of the victim in 'compromising' positions and these were posted online.[34] One judge stated that he could not continue to review some of the recordings describing the material as 'disgusting'.[35]

The harm caused to the victim(s)

There are short-, medium- and long-term consequences to child sexual abuse for victims, their family members and society.[36] Research on the impact of child sexual abuse has established a wide range of physical, emotional and psychological effects for victims.[37] The consequences and impact will differ depending on the victim, the nature of the offending and the relationship between the parties.[38] Studies examining the long-term effects of child sexual abuse demonstrate that victims may have a lower rate of psychological wellbeing, a lower socio-economic status as well as a higher likelihood of multiple victimisations when compared with non-victims.[39]

The harm caused to victims was directly expressed as an aggravating factor by sentencing judges in all cases. Judges emphasised the severity of the consequences arising from the offending, resulting in victims being 'severely traumatised'[40] and 'seriously scarred'.[41] Judges were informed of the harm caused through an assessment of the facts of the case as well as the evidence presented by expert witnesses at the sentencing hearing, including from psychologists and psychiatrists. Victim impact statements were valued by judges in assessing the harm caused and they were identified in 77.7 per cent of cases (49 of 63). Judges commended victims on providing this information to the court noting that it required 'great courage and resilience' in submitting and delivering these statements.[42] Such was the gravity and breadth of the offending, that judges acknowledged that the sentence imposed could never reflect the level of harm caused to the victims. One judge noted the 'sad and moving evidence' provided by the victims while another stated that the experience of the abuse 'rendered [the victims] lives little short of a permanent crucifixion'.[43]

The physical harm caused was well documented in these cases and this was also connected with the negative consequences in terms of the victims' mental health, wellbeing and relationships. For example, a judge noted that the victim had been left with 'cauliflower ear' as well as scars and deformed nails from the offending.[44] The victim described how the offender kicked, hit and slapped her and that she was ashamed to go to school because of the noticeable marks and bruises. A psychologist testified that the victim had been living in overwhelming fear and felt that if she confided in anyone her father would kill her. The court heard the offending had undermined her trust in adults, had negatively impacted her relationship with her mother and left her with an overwhelming sense of shame and powerlessness.

Sentencing judges noted and took into consideration evidence from victims, and other witnesses, of the impact the offending had on their mental health and emotional wellbeing. Describing the long-term effects of the offending, a clinical psychologist at a sentencing hearing stated that the memory of the abuse would continue for the rest of the victims' lives. In a further case, the court heard that the victim had gone from a happy, fun-loving child to a child with severe depression. Feelings of shame and isolation were frequently expressed by victims with one victim stating: 'I trusted my dad. He was my hero growing up. I always felt it was my fault and I was ashamed of myself'.[45] A range of mental health diagnoses, such as anxiety and depression, were referenced by judges as a consequence of the offending behaviour. Suicidal ideation emerged as an impact of child sexual abuse with victims informing the court that they had suicidal thoughts in the aftermath of the offending and some victims had attempted suicide.

The impact of the offending on the victims' existing relationships and potential future relationships was documented in the assessment of the harm caused. Victims of intrafamilial abuse tend to experience greater negative effects than those victimised by a non-relative.[46] Given the intrafamilial abuse prevalent in these cases, the ramifications for the life course of the victim cannot be understated. One victim described that she 'could never call her father "dad" again'.[47] A judge, having heard testimony from the victim (the daughter of the defendant), stated: 'the only way I could assuage her terror' was to impose long-term imprisonment.[48] In another case, the judge noted that a victim, abused by his step-father, was now living in residential care and that the child 'feels like a dog that nobody wants'.[49] Harm was also identified in the context of the difficulties victims encountered in forming trusting relationships as a result of the offending, with some victims expressing that they felt 'unworthy of love'.[50] In addition to assessing the gravity of the offence and the harm caused to the victim, judges also referenced factors more directly related to the offender.

Assessing the offender

Similar to cases involving adult victims, all of the perpetrators in these cases were male. Establishing the age of the offender at the time of offending was difficult as there was a delay in the reporting in many of these cases and the perpetrators were committing offences over a prolonged period. A factor of significant relevance was the previous criminal history of the offender. In cases involving child victims, previous criminal history was referenced in almost one third of cases (31.7 per cent or 20 of 63). The offender had been convicted of a sexual offence in just over half of these cases (55 per cent or 11 of 20). There were two cases where the offender had previously been convicted of the rape of a child. Offenders also had previous convictions for non-sexual offences (55 per cent or 11 of 20) and these included a wide range of offences, from the most serious to the minor level (including: murder; assault; robbery; burglary; theft; and road traffic offences). In three cases the offender had previously been convicted of both sexual and non-sexual offences.

Although the prevalence of previous criminal sexual history is technically lower than in cases involving adults (see Chapter 4), this needs to be understood in the broader context of the volume of offending, the multitude of victims and the extended period of time during which the offending took place. In sentencing generally, the absence of previous criminal history may operate to the benefit of the defendant in terms of mitigation as it is interpreted as evidence of good character. But, given the multiplicity of offending in these cases, the absence of previous criminal history is, as one judge pointed out, 'hardly indicative of good character'.[51] As such, there was little evidence that a lack of previous criminal history contributed to a positive assessment of character, resulting in a reduction in sentence.

These cases are complicated in the sense that there may be a delay in the reporting of sexual abuse and where there are multiple victims, the victims may report to the authorities at different times or at the same time. This could mean that all of the offences are heard together or there may be multiple sentencing hearings for multiple offences committed against multiple victims a number of years previously. Consequently, previous criminal history may not be reflective of the chronological order of offending. For example, a judge noted that an offender had 42 previous convictions including a 15-year sentence for multiple rapes and sexual assaults of a girl over a six-year period. These offences actually occurred after the commission of the offences for which he was currently being sentenced, as there was a delay in reporting these crimes to the authorities. There were also instances where there were multiple different sentencing hearings for child sexual abuse perpetrated against multiple victims during the same period. For example, a man sentenced to 18 years' imprisonment for the rape and sexual abuse of his daughter over a 13-year period was, at the time of sentencing, already serving an eight-year sentence for sexual offences committed against two of his other daughters during the same period. This sentence had been imposed the previous year. Given that many offenders were committing offences over an extended period of time, assertions from the defendant regarding a lack of previous criminal history in support of mitigation did not appear to gain much traction with sentencing judges.

The risk of reoffending

Although there were identifiable expressions of concern regarding the risk of reoffending and public protection, it was a factor that was less frequently highlighted by judges in cases of child sexual abuse (20.6 per cent or 13 of 63) when compared with cases involving adult victims. The risk of reoffending was more frequently discernable in extrafamilial child sexual abuse cases (61.5 per cent or eight of 13). A meta-analysis comparing intra- and extrafamilial child sexual abuse showed that extrafamilial offenders are at a higher risk of reoffending when compared with intrafamilial offenders.[52] Research on risk factors show that antisocial sexual interests and atypical sexual interests are more prevalent in extra- rather intrafamilial sex offenders.[53] In addition, the specific familial circumstances where the offending exists are unlikely to arise again and this may impact the risk of reoffending.[54] The evidence from the analysis of the cases highlights that the risk of reoffending is informed through professional assessments made available to the court as well as being informed through the offence itself and the previous criminal history of the offender. It may be the case that sentencing remarks referring to risk are shaped by the assessments and decisions provided by experts and this can help account for the differences in risk-related commentary in relation to intra- and extrafamilial cases. In determinate sentence cases, where the risk of reoffending was identified as a factor, the court regularly imposed a post-release supervision order as a means of dealing with risk.

Assessing mitigating factors

Given the severity of the penalty in these cases and the rarity of imposing a sentence of this length, it is clear that if mitigation arose, its impact was limited. There were only a small number of cases (6.4 per cent or 4 of 63) where the judge explicitly stated that were no mitigating factors in the case. In three quarter of cases (74.6 per cent or 47 of 63) references to mitigating factors by the sentencing judge were identified.[55] Where it was possible to identify a numerical reduction as a result of mitigation, the reduction from the headline sentence ranged from one to seven years, with over three quarters of cases seeing a reduction of between one to three years

(79.2 per cent or 19 of 24). Given the seriousness and volume of offending, offence-related mitigation did not arise. Instead, there was a focus on the response to charges (such as the guilty plea) or personal mitigation (such as age).

The guilty plea was the central factor in gaining a reduction in sentence but cooperation with the authorities at an early stage was also important. A guilty plea was entered by the defendant in 44 of 63 cases (69.8 per cent).[56] As discussed in Chapter 4, the stage at which a guilty plea is entered impacts the likelihood and level of discount. The plea was entered at the first reasonable opportunity in most cases (60 per cent or 18 of 30).[57] The remainder of defendants entered a plea post charge but before the trial (26.7 per cent or eight of 30) or during the trial (13.3 per cent or four of 30). A typical example would be a case where an offender entered a guilty plea at the first reasonable opportunity, resulting in a reduction of three years. But a reduction in sentence was not necessarily guaranteed and there were numerous examples where sentencing judges did not apply a discount where they determined that the offending was exceptionally serious and/or the guilty plea was entered late in the process (see Chapter 6). A guilty plea described as coming at 'the 11th hour' did not result in a reduction in sentence.[58]

Expressions of remorse was cited as a mitigating factor (25.4 per cent or 16 of 63). A lack of remorse as well as the conduct of the defendant throughout the criminal process could also operate to demonstrate the absence of mitigation and in one instance this was viewed as aggravating. A sentencing judge pointed to the offender's lack of 'genuine remorse', attempt to sabotage the trial process and 'smart alecky' attitude as counting as aggravating factors.[59] There were cases where the court was presented with evidence relating to the physical and mental health of the offender and/or their physical or intellectual disabilities although the impact of this was minimal. In one case, the court was presented with evidence that the defendant had been diagnosed with 'paranoid psychosis' and was in the

Central Mental Hospital at the time of sentencing.[60] The sentencing judge acknowledged the mental health diagnosis but stated that this was a 'very small mitigating factor'.[61] Willingness to engage with psychological services and a sex offender therapy programme was also identified as a relevant mitigating factor in one case as it demonstrated a pathway to rehabilitation.

There is a practice in Irish sentencing whereby offenders present evidence to establish 'good character' through witnesses or documentary evidence. This might emphasise the offender's employment record, work ethic and/or positive contribution to the community. There are legitimate questions regarding the role and relevance of 'good character' in the context of sentencing, particularly in cases of child sexual abuse. In England and Wales, sentencing guidelines for serious sex offences states that good character or exemplary conduct does not justify a reduction in sentence.[62] In practice, there was little evidence to indicate that 'good character' was being applied by sentencing judges to reduce a sentence across cases involving both adult and child victims. In one case the sentencing judge acknowledged that the defendant had outwardly been a 'paragon of virtue' in his volunteering and community activities but, at the same time, had been sexually abusing his daughter.[63] The judge did not reduce the sentence on the basis of the offender's volunteering or work commitments.

The age of the offender arose as a factor for consideration in a number of cases. Although the offences were rarely committed by elderly persons, there was a cohort of offenders that were elderly at the time of sentencing as there was a delay in reporting in some cases. The rationale for applying mitigation for those who are elderly is an acknowledgement of the reality that each year in custody represents a significantly greater proportion of the offender's lifetime when compared with a younger person.[64] There was some evidence that the age of the offender resulted in a reduction in sentence although that reduction was moderate. A three-year discount was applied in a case due to the combined mitigating factors of the defendant's advanced years (71 at the time of sentencing) and lack of previous convictions. Another judge reduced a sentence from life imprisonment to 20 years on account of the offender's age (75 at the time of sentencing).

Selecting life imprisonment

A total of 12 cases resulted in a sentence of life imprisonment and an analysis indicates some distinctions from determinate sentences in terms of the prevalence of certain factors. For example, three quarters involved multiple victims where life sentences were imposed as opposed to half of determinate sentence cases. A previous criminal history was identified in half of the cases where life imprisonment was imposed and these included serious sexual and non-sexual offences (rape, child abduction, aggravated burglary and robbery). Cases did not tend to involve any significant disparities in terms of the volume of offences when compared with determinate sentences. In a case where the Court of Appeal increased a 15-year sentence to life imprisonment, the court noted that consecutive sentences had not been imposed and that the offending (orchestrated by the defendant in concert with other family members against his young and vulnerable children) needed to be viewed in its totality and reflected in the sentence. In other cases, it was sometimes difficult to discern the difference between life sentence and determinate sentence cases when assessing the degree of violence, culpability of the offender or the harm to the victim. Interestingly, there was a higher rate of guilty pleas with 10 out of 12 of those that pleaded guilty being sentenced to life imprisonment.

Delay and the evolving responses to child sexual abuse

There are many barriers victims experience that may delay the disclosure of child sexual abuse including: their relationship with the abuser; the demands of the abuser; and social pressures and attitudes to child sexual abuse.[65] Ring, a leading scholar on child sexual abuse, notes that Irish society played a significant role in maintaining a culture of silence surrounding these crimes, particularly during the twentieth century.[66] All of these factors impact the agency of victims to seek justice through the legal process. In addition, legal barriers may impact the likelihood of child sexual abuse cases being successfully prosecuted. The courts' response to cases where there was a delay in the disclosure of child sexual abuse significantly shaped the likelihood of these cases being prosecuted and appearing before a judge for sentencing. The approach by the courts to the issue of delay in the disclosure of abuse, and its impact on the defendant's right to a fair trial, has evolved over the course of this study. Up until the mid-2000s, a relatively stringent approach was adopted, with the issue of delay often being dealt with by way of a pre-trial appeal. The courts, in assessing whether the delay infringed the defendant's right to a fair trial, tended to focus on the victim's reasons for not reporting the offending.[67] Currently, delay is dealt with by the trial judge and the focus is on the risk of an unfair trial.[68]

In this study, many victim(s) decided to disclose their experiences of child sexual abuse to the authorities in adulthood. In 24 cases (38.1 per cent) it was possible to identify a period of five years or more from the commission of the last offence to the victim accessing the criminal justice system. There were six cases where there was a delay of 20 years or more. It was not always possible to measure the delay in reporting and so this is an underestimation of delay in these cases. A study conducted of child sexual abuse cases during 2005 to 2012 found an interval of 10 years or more from the date of the first offence to the date of sentence in 80 per cent of cases.[69] Sentencing in these cases is complex as judges must take account of the offender's circumstances at the time of offending as well as at the time of sentencing.[70]

There was strong evidence of the social and personal barriers that influence the likelihood of disclosure in victim impact statements. In particular, there were many instances of the offender using threats, coercion and control to ensure that the victim did not disclose the offending to a third party. Given that the perpetrator was a father (or step-father) in a large number of these cases, the perpetrator exploited this position to exert control over the victim. There were also cases where victims stated that they did not understand as children that the abuse was criminal in nature at the time. Offenders who were deemed to be of good character or holding certain esteem in the community also impacted the ability of the victim to disclose the sexual abuse at the time of offending or thereafter. Indeed, there were instances where the victim(s) did disclose the abuse at the time but were not believed by those they trusted. A victim disclosed to his parents that he was being sexually abused by a priest during the 1970s and 1980s. The parents responded by beating the child and saying: 'How could you say that about a man of God?'[71] The priest continued to abuse this child and other children following this disclosure. The victim reported the crimes to the authorities over 20 years later. It is important to acknowledge that there are a multitude of factors, actors and forces that may funnel cases towards or away from a sentencing court at any given time. As a result, sentencing decisions can be reflective of the wider social, legal and political landscape.

Conclusion

There is a consistency evident in the picture created through the analysis of these cases. In terms of identifiable factors that impact the imposition of the use of the upper range of the penalty, it is clear that in cases involving child victims there are a number of central factors. These include the age of the victim, the relationship between the parties, the prolonged period of offending, the number of offences, the number of victims and the use of special violence, degradation and humiliation. The harm caused to the victim(s) was of great importance in elevating the sentencing outcome into the most serious band. Even in circumstances where there were mitigating factors, these had a limited impact on the sentence outcome. At times, judges acknowledged the sentence length imposed in these cases could not adequately reflect the gravity of the offending or the harm caused given the sheer volume of offences. It is difficult to resolve this issue in a way that meets the need for public disapprobation while taking into account principle and practice. It is undoubtedly the case that offenders being sentenced for multiple offences often committed against multiple victims are effectively receiving the benefit of a bulk discount by virtue of all of these offences being dealt with at the same sentencing hearing. This is facilitated through the practice of imposing concurrent rather than consecutive sentences. Were these offences to be dealt with at separate hearings held over a staggered period of time, the offender would end up serving significantly longer in prison. One method of addressing this was to impose an indeterminate sentence of life imprisonment in exceptionally serious cases. The next chapter assesses how judges, their practical wisdom, and occupational environment can contribute to sentencing outcomes.

SIX

Factoring in judges

Introduction

Given the broad discretion afforded judges, it is certainly conceivable that the individual making the decision may be an important factor to consider when analysing sentencing outcomes. When a sentence is criticised for perceived inconsistency or disparity it is usually the judge that becomes the focus of the public's ire. The role that the individual can play in arriving at a decision will, in some ways, be dependent on the level of discretion or constraint afforded to that decision-maker. When discretion is unfettered, the individual themselves may become a factor that contributes to the outcome.[1] As documented thus far, while judicial discretion is wide, decision-making is shaped by a 'sentencing canon' of appellate judgments, legislative constraints and judicial practice.

In this chapter, the role of the judge and the impact of the environment within which they operate offers additional insights into the consistency in sentencing factors discussed in previous chapters. Evidence of the 'practical wisdom' used to arrive at a decision is examined. A broader analysis of sentencing remarks demonstrates that judges are not just concerned with following the principle of proportionality for their colleagues to scrutinise on appeal, they must also convey a sentencing message to a wider audience. Sentences of this severity are regularly appealed and the influence of the appeals process is explored in terms of its direct impact on outcomes as well as the development of sentencing policy. The chapter also expands the frame of analysis to look at some of the social, political and legal influences operating within the sentencing ecosystem. An example from the 1990s explores how the rumblings of judges and public concern regarding the guilty plea discount pressured politicians to pursue legislative reform that had an impact on sentencing practice.

The sentencing environment

To understand the consistency evident in these cases, the environment within which they were decided must also be analysed. The occupational setting as well as the routines and roles of actors occupying this space are critical to decision-making.[2] In Ireland, sentencing decisions for serious sexual offences are decided by the judges of the Central Criminal Court (the High Court when it is hearing a criminal case).[3] The Court functions with one judge presiding, and when there is a trial, it is by jury. The Court sits in one building in Dublin, Ireland's capital city, but over the last decade or so it has operated from different cities around the country on occasion. The Central Criminal Court has exclusive jurisdiction of rape offences and aggravated sexual assault (as well as murder, attempted murder, piracy, genocide and some competition offences). In practice, sexual offence cases have become the main sentencing workload of judges of the Central Criminal Court. In 2023, 92 per cent of sentencing offences resolved by the Central Criminal Court related to sexual offences.[4] Another offence dealt with by the Court is murder but, in terms of sentencing, due to the mandatory nature of the life sentence for this offence, judges have no discretion in these cases. Judges of this court will overwhelmingly be exercising their sentencing discretion in sexual offence cases.

The knowledge base accrued through this is likely to increase the 'practical wisdom' in decision-making and embed the consistency of approach. The rarity of such serious cases appearing before the courts also increases the likelihood of consistency in approach and outcome.

The personnel of the Court has changed over the decades. For a period up until the 2000s, it was reported that there was only one permanent judge assigned to the Central Criminal Court, with other judges being assigned to cases occasionally.[5] By 2021, there could be ten different judges dealing with cases in the Central Criminal Court at any given time.[6] In this study, a total of 24 judges were responsible for sentencing outcomes in 108 cases. One judge was responsible for almost half of these sentencing outcomes (45 per cent or 49 of 108). This judge, Mr Justice Paul Carney, became a controversial figure in Irish criminal justice during his time at the Central Criminal Court. He was responsible for over two thirds of the sentencing outcomes where 15 years to life imprisonment was imposed during his tenure at the Court (49 of 71 cases from 1991 to March 2015).

It is difficult to ascertain to what extent 'the character' of the judge played a role in these sentencing outcomes. He was the main judge dealing with cases at this level at the time and it would be speculative to state that had there been more diversity in personnel that sentencing outcomes may have been different. Nonetheless, his controversial and outspoken approach was well documented by the media, reporting on his 'provocative remarks during extra-judicial outings and his thinly and not so thinly veiled attacks on the Court of Criminal Appeal'.[7] He was certainly an outlier in this regard, given that his contemporaries rarely engaged in public comment. In terms of understanding the consistent patterns and factors in the preceding analysis of cases, this judge undoubtedly played a role in shaping that picture and in embedding the sentencing factors for future decision-makers. From 2015 onwards, sentencing decisions were made by a wider pool of judges and this can be attributed to a growth in the number of judges specifically assigned to the Court. These decisions did not depart, to any great extent, from the profile of cases decided during the Carney era.

The regularity with which judges deal with sexual offence cases and the small number of judges involved cannot be left out of the conversation in understanding sentencing patterns. Other sexual offences, alongside most other offences, are dealt with in courts across the country in either the District Court or Circuit Court. As a result, sentencing outcomes for these offences are the responsibility of a much bigger pool of judges who have a very diverse caseload. It is unlikely that similar levels of consistency are being replicated across the wide range of sexual offence cases appearing before judges for sentencing up and down the country.

Sentencing decisions are not taken in isolation but are reliant upon prior decisions and judgments made at earlier stages of the process.[8] As outlined in Chapter 2, the information presented to the judge at the sentencing hearing is largely determined and shaped by non-judicial actors, who construct the facts of the case and the factors of relevance.[9] Sentencing decisions should therefore be understood as the product of a collaborative process.[10] Judges are heavily reliant on the quality of information presented to them and, as such, these parties play an important role in shaping decisions. These roles can evolve and judges have been keen to secure greater information and guidance, particularly from the Director of Public Prosecutions (the DPP). For example, prosecutors traditionally viewed their role as being neutral and they generally do not advocate for a specific sentence or sentence range to be imposed.[11] In 2014, the Court of Criminal Appeal stated that this position could no longer be justified, particularly given the growth in guidance and structure around sentencing.[12] There is no reason as to why a sentencing judge should not be in receipt of information relevant to situating the offending into a sentencing range and the DPP should provide 'real assistance' to the judge in this respect.[13] The Supreme Court has expressed similar sentiments.[14]

The introduction of a procedure (in the 1990s) whereby the prosecution can appeal a sentence believed to be unduly lenient led to the 'feeling' among trial and appellate judges that it is no longer sustainable for the DPP to retain a passive approach on the sentence to be imposed.[15] Despite this, the DPP has continued to try to stick to its more neutral role. Their latest set of guidelines for prosecutors state that it is not appropriate for a prosecutor to submit a band or range of sentence to the judge unless the appellate courts have already issued a judgment providing sentencing bands.[16] Guidance on sentencing bands have been issued for some offences in Ireland but this is still fairly limited. This dispute shows that the roles participants play in a sentencing hearing are fluid and may evolve over time as expectations change.

Practical wisdom – personal and professional

In the search for aggravating and mitigating factors in sentencing remarks, the wider ranging and less tangible influences on sentencing practice can be overlooked. The knowledge of a judge, obtained through many years of legal and personal experience, is an important contributing factor in a discretionary sentencing system. This is sometimes referred to as the 'practical wisdom' of the judge and is often put forward as an argument for the retention of discretion. The role of the judge in employing their professional experience, intuition and subjective judgement in sentencing has been acknowledged by the Court of Appeal.[17] This type of knowledge is 'tacit, unspecified and internal' and is not easily systematised through a sentencing guideline.[18] Nor is its impact on sentencing outcomes easy to measure. Some argue that structuring discretion or putting a more formalised system in place can jeopardise this important factor in sentencing.[19] But even in jurisdictions where there are guidelines, it cannot be assumed that these rules will be applied consistently by sentencers. They may still be mediated through the 'practical wisdom' of the decision-maker.[20] The judge will always play some role in the outcome.

In terms of the evidence of 'practical wisdom' in sentencing remarks, judges regularly employed their own legal and professional experiences as a barometer in measuring the exceptional nature of the offending. Many judges articulated that the case was the 'most difficult' and 'most horrendous' of their time on the bench.[21] Indeed, over half of the judges in this study had only one case where they imposed a sentence in the top range during the period under review (13 of 24). One judge described the offending as 'the most grievous sexual assault I have ever come across in my career'.[22] Others made similar references in assessing seriousness and expressing abhorrence: 'In my 40 years of practice … I have never heard of a more brutal crime'.[23] Appellate judges were not immune to the impact of the seriousness of these crimes expressing 'outrage' and 'disgust' in relation to the level of offending.[24] Appellate judges described the offending as the 'worst … that had come before the court' as far back as the judges of the court could remember.[25] Using professional experiences as an indicator of seriousness was a means of gauging and communicating the exceptional and extreme nature of the sexual violence.

There was also evidence that the offending evoked a more personal assessment and response. Some of the language used in sentencing remarks indicated that the offending provoked a visceral reaction from sentencing judges (see Chapters 4 and 5). Many judges expressed that the facts of the case were 'almost unbelievable'.[26] Such was the extremity of violence, one judge stated that the video material was 'so disgusting, that I, as a judge who handles some 140 cases a year, could not go through with more than 10 minutes of it'.[27] This language was regularly used as an alternative to describing the facts of the offending in granular detail, something judges expressed as being difficult and challenging for them in the discharging of their duties. As one judge noted: 'The facts of this case are unspeakable, and I cannot bring myself to repeat them'.[28] There remains a taboo surrounding the articulation of the reality of serious sexual offending, particularly when it involves vulnerable parties, such as children. At times it appeared that judges utilised emotive and provocative language to convey the seriousness of the offending without engaging in a detailed description of it.

Judges are often expected to repress emotions in the performance of their duties or, at the very least, employ a different suite of emotions than would be expected as a personal response or a response in a different vocational setting.[29] The analysis in this study reveals fissures in this façade, with judges expressing themselves in an unusually personalised manner when remarking on the gravity of the offence and the harm to the victims(s). This emotive language identified in sentencing remarks may be serving a wider purpose. Sentencing remarks are not just a means of communicating to judicial colleagues and criminal justice professionals. They must communicate the sentencing message to victims, defendants, the media and the public.[30] This is why, as Tata observes, there can be a certain level of incoherency to sentencing remarks.[31] These remarks are not simply a record of the application of the rules to the facts but may also be reflective of the broader pressures within and outside the courtroom to deliver a message to audiences with varying expectations.

Recalibrating sentencing

As discussed in Chapter 2, appellate courts have played a critical role in developing principles that influence sentencing practice. The 'sentencing canon' of appellate decisions set precedent for future decisions and the appellate courts have become increasingly active in issuing judgments on a whole range of sentencing matters. There have been major developments in judicial guidance on sentencing in recent years. In terms of sexual offences, the guidance judgment for rape was issued by the Supreme Court towards the end of this study (2019). An earlier decision in 2007 by the Central Criminal Court, which detailed sentencing bands based on existing practice, although not binding precedent, was clearly influential on subsequent decisions at trial and on appeal.[32] There has been a noticeable increase in the level of clarity and detail in sentencing remarks over the last decade when analysing these cases and greater guidance on sentencing procedures from the appellate courts have undoubtedly contributed to this. Legal scholars tend to focus their analysis on the development of precedent at appellate level and there is an ever-expanding volume of judgments articulating principles that are of relevance to the work of sentencing judges. Yet, we know very little about whether these principles are being effectively transmitted to sentencing judges and how these principles are integrated into sentencing deliberations.[33] To gain some further perspective on the dynamics between the trial and appellate courts, it is useful to explore the direct and oblique impacts arising from appellate decisions.

The appellate process performs a critical oversight function that can recalibrate sentencing outcomes. The decision of the appellate court will have a direct impact on the final sentence outcome and, ultimately, the sentence that will be served. The sentence imposed at the hearing may prove to be the end of the legal process for some. But in this study, it was possible to identify an appeal in 51 per cent of cases (55 of 108), the majority of which involved an appeal against sentence (46 of 55 cases).[34] The Court of Appeal (and formerly the Court of Criminal Appeal prior to 2014) deals with appeals against sentence from the Central Criminal Court. The Court of Appeal consists of three judges. In deciding an appeal against a sentence, the Court may uphold, increase, reduce or vary the sentence in some manner. A decision may be appealed to the Supreme Court where the Court certifies that the case involves a point of law of exceptional public importance and it is in the public interest that it be heard by the Supreme Court.[35]

Similar to the sentencing court, the appellate court has considerable discretion in terms of how, and to what extent (if at all), the sentence is increased or decreased. In making a determination, a sentence should not be reduced or increased solely on the basis that the judges of the appellate court would have dealt with it differently had they been the sentencing judge.[36] In fact, the appellate court adopts a deferential position to the sentencing court on the basis that the judge is in a better position than the appellate court to determine the gravity of the offence and circumstances of the offender. The court must identify an error of principle arising in the original sentence in order to alter that sentence. An error of principle could be, for example, the failure to properly account for a mitigating factor, such as a guilty plea. It may also arise where the sentencing judge has not exercised their discretion judiciously or where the sentence exceeded the appropriate boundaries for an offence of this nature.[37] For example, in a Supreme Court case decided in 1994, the Court disagreed with the judge's sentencing remarks that this was 'the worst case to come before the Central Criminal Court'.[38] The Supreme Court, describing the sentence as 'excessive', noted that the 'very extreme view taken by the learned trial judge undoubtedly coloured his assessment of the appropriate sentences'.[39]

Defendants that appealed against the severity of sentence had a 50:50 success rate in securing a reduction in sentence (see Table 6.1). Since 1993, the DPP is empowered to appeal a sentence that they believe to be unduly lenient.[40]

Table 6.1: Outcome of appeals against sentence severity

Appeal outcomes	Cases involving adult victims	Cases involving child victims
Uphold sentence	9	12
Reduce sentence	9	12

The DPP has remarked that applications of undue leniency where a sentence of 15 years has been imposed by the sentencing judge would be 'far and few between'.[41] There were four cases where the DPP appealed on the basis of undue leniency and three of these applications resulted in an increase in sentence. In 2024, the Court of Appeal increased the sentences of co-defendants who committed offences of rape, sexual exploitation and child cruelty against five young children.[42] The Court increased the sentence of the father of the children from 15 years to life imprisonment and increased the sentence of the uncle from 15 years to 18.5 years. In addition to the factors referenced by the sentencing judge (including prolonged abuse, betrayal of trust, neglect, and the control exerted by the defendants) the Court noted additional aggravating factors arising from the manipulative and deceitful interactions with social workers and how they collectively exploited these young children trapped within a family of abusers. In another case the structure of the sentence was changed but the overall sentence length was not.

Appellate judges overwhelmingly confirmed the assessment by the sentencing judge that the offending was in the top range in terms of seriousness. This was the case irrespective of whether the sentence was upheld or reduced. In upholding the sentence imposed in half of these appeals, appellate judges confirmed that the offending was 'extreme',[43] of the 'utmost gravity'[44] and at 'the very highest point'[45] of the range of offending. Similarly, where a sentence was reduced the seriousness of the offence was rarely a factor of significance with the Court describing the offending as of the 'utmost barbarity',[46] 'extremely' and 'extraordinarily' serious[47] and 'appalling in its ferocity'.[48] In cases where a reduction was secured primarily or in part due to an error in assessing offence seriousness, it did not necessarily result in a reduction below the band of 15 years to life imprisonment. One life sentence was reduced to 16 years on the basis that the offending was not at the level of seriousness warranting the ultimate penalty.

A failure on the part of the sentencing judge to account or give sufficient credit for a mitigating factor (or factors) was the most frequently cited error of principle that resulted in a reduction in sentence. In over half of the cases where the sentence was reduced, the appellate court determined that insufficient weight was attached to the guilty plea and a greater discount was required. A failure to incorporate a rehabilitative component in the sentence arose as a rationale for reduction in a number of cases. A programme of rehabilitation presented at sentencing appears to be valuable in seeking a reduction in sentence on appeal, although the submission needs to be credible.[49] In one case, a life sentence was reduced primarily on the basis of the progress the defendant had made in terms of rehabilitation since the offending. The Court of Appeal viewed this as moving the offending out of the life imprisonment category and imposed a determinate sentence instead. There was a plethora of other errors of principle identified that may have operated singularly or in conjunction with other factors that contributed to a reduction in sentence (for example: previous criminal history; preventative detention; and dysfunctional background).

Overall, appellate judges were inclined to give more weight to mitigating factors than sentencing judges. Of course, there are many possible explanations for this but part of it might relate to the different environments within which these decisions are made. Trial judges hear the evidence of this egregious offending in court and deliver sentencing remarks in front of the victim, defendant, the media and the public. Appellate judges operate more on a paper basis through reviewing written submissions and court transcripts as well as oral arguments from barristers. There is more distance from the 'visceral' evidence in the trial court and the public-facing nature of sentencing.

A system of oversight may also have a more indirect impact on the formulation and articulation of the sentence. In deliberating and communicating their decisions, judges are aware that their remarks are likely to be scrutinised on appeal (by their judicial colleagues). This is even more pronounced in these cases as decisions are made by a very small group of judges sentencing serious sexual offence cases. There is an ongoing feedback loop in operation as a result of the regular flow of decisions being made and reviewed. As a result, sentencing judges may tend to adopt a defensible approach to their decision-making through adhering to the frameworks and principles previously established by the appellate courts. Defensible decisions are those that can be defended in hindsight when being scrutinised at a later date.[50] This can be achieved through the application of the rules or regulations and through grounding the decision in the available evidence.[51] This provides the decision-maker with a sense of security rendering their decision-making defensible while also mitigating some of the responsibility for the decision. The idea and prospect of oversight and accountability may serve as a constraint on sentencing deliberations and remarks. The downside is that it may also have the effect of widening the gap between the 'real' reasons for the decision in the judges' mind and the reasons for the decision as articulated in their sentencing remarks. Having demonstrated how decisions may be influenced by their environment, work practices and institutional structures, it is worth considering other layers of influence operating outside or alongside this sentencing echo chamber. An example from the 1990s demonstrates the role other agents can play in shaping sentencing policy and practice.

Guilty pleas and social unease

While the actions of and relationship between trial and appellate judges are central to understanding sentencing outcomes, there are also broader social, political and legal influences of relevance. The guilty plea discount debate that emerged in the 1990s provides a good example of how sentencing issues can spill out into the public domain, can be captured by other agents and may result in real changes to sentencing practice. Returning to the *Tiernan* decision discussed in Chapter 2, the Supreme Court reduced a sentence from 21 to 17 years primarily to account properly for the guilty plea.[52] This 1980s' judgment drove the idea of developing offence-specific guidance into the legal wilderness for many years. It also cemented the concept that a guilty plea required a reduction in sentence even in the most serious sexual offence cases. During the 1990s, a number of decisions sparked controversy as a result of perceived leniency, not simply in relation to the sentence imposed, but the tendency of the appellate courts to reduce these sentences when appealed.[53] The guilty plea played a central role in these reductions. This led to frustration expressed by sentencing judges, politicians and the public, and culminated in legislative change.

In 1991, an offender was sentenced to 12 concurrent life sentences for the sexual abuse of three children over a six-year period. This sentence was subsequently reduced by the Supreme Court to 15 years primarily on the basis of a guilty plea entered at an early stage.[54] The Supreme Court noted that the fact that the maximum sentence was imposed across the offences meant that the guilty plea had not been properly taken into consideration. During the same period, one of the most significant and high-profile Irish cases, popularly known as '*the X case*', came before the courts. *X* was a 14-year-old girl who became pregnant as a result of being sexually abused by *Z*. There were two significant judgments that resulted. A Supreme Court ruling decided issues of constitutional importance related to the right to access an abortion.[55] There was also a criminal prosecution dealing with *Z*'s offences. At sentencing, the judge described the defendant as 'depraved and evil' when imposing a 14-year sentence.[56] On appeal, the sentence was reduced to four years, partly on the basis of a guilty plea. This decision sparked widespread media commentary and public outrage at the reduction in sentence as well as criticism of statements by the appellate court that the defendant was a 'hard-working, good family man … who had surfaced from humble origins to a position of some affluence'.[57]

These decisions created tension between sentencing judges and the appellate courts and, at times, this spilled into sentencing remarks. The matter came to a head in 1995, when Mr Justice Paul Carney voiced frustration at not being able to impose his preferred sentence of life imprisonment so as to reflect the 'heinousness and multiplicity' of offending against ten child victims.[58] The offender had pleaded guilty to 27 offences, a sample of the 210 offences originally on the indictment. The judge stated that a sentence of life imprisonment was 'not open' to him as a result of the binding decisions of the appellate courts on the guilty plea discount.[59] Indeed, at the time, some sentencing remarks from this judge were openly critical of decisions of the Court of Criminal Appeal. As a result, and amidst growing public unease regarding sentencing, the then Minister for Justice raised concern at the limitations being placed on sentencing judges and indicated that these would be removed by legislation, if possible.[60]

The matter was ultimately addressed by the legislature *via* the Criminal Justice Act 1999. The Act permits a court to impose a maximum sentence notwithstanding a guilty plea where the judge is satisfied that there are such exceptional circumstances relating to the offence to warrant such a penalty.[61] This legislative change does appear to have had an impact on decisions at both trial and appellate level. Post legislative reform, the appellate courts upheld eight cases where a judge imposed a sentence of life imprisonment even where there was a guilty plea. The rationale for upholding these sentences despite a guilty plea was related to the exceptional seriousness of the offending. The Supreme Court stated that 'a maximum sentence might be warranted notwithstanding a plea' in rare cases.[62] There is a question as to whether legislative reform was required in the first place. The Supreme Court, as far back as 1987, had stated that there could be no principle which inhibited the imposition of a lawful sentence merely because the defendant had entered a guilty plea.[63] This would include a maximum sentence. Yet, it is clear that this was not apparent to sentencing judges during the intervening years nor did it sway the appellate courts to uphold these sentences until legislation on the matter was adopted.

The resolution of the disjoint between sentencing judges and the appellate courts through legislation as a result of a wider discussion and debate is evidence of the democratic function that sentencing plays in the exchange of ideas around the legitimacy and purposes of punishment.[64] Curiously, and despite public pressure on politicians regarding sentencing, there has been limited use of legislation when it comes to developing sentencing procedures and rules. Commentators have noted resistance by judges to legislative reform that makes inroads on judicial discretion and this may explain the hands-off approach.[65] Academics have consistently highlighted the dangers of reforms arising from public debate on criminal justice issues and the tendency of these to be populist and punitive.[66] That being said, there are examples that some legislative reforms have been well received by judges in the sentencing domain.

Victim impact statements, adopted by legislation in 1993, have become common practice in sentencing and they were referred to in 76.5 per cent of cases decided from 1993 onwards (75 of 98).[67] This legislation was introduced following public outcry arising from a case where the defendant received a suspended sentence for rape. Lavinia Kerwick waived her right to anonymity as a victim and campaigned for this important legislative change.[68] Her case and campaign work also contributed to legislative change that permits the DPP to appeal sentences that they believe to be unduly lenient. In 2001, legislation provided for a series of notification and supervision orders that were designed to manage sex offenders in the community. Judges regularly imposed a post-release supervision order in addition to a determinate sentence. Since 1997, a judge is required to treat as aggravating an offender that commits an offence while on bail for a pre-existing charge.[69] This type of case did not appear frequently in the study, although there was evidence of this being considered as an aggravating factor with the legislation being referenced.[70] These reforms do not curtail discretion to any great degree. Legislation is a tool that has been under-utilised in framing sentencing in Ireland and the evidence presented here suggests that judges are open to this type of legislative direction. The creation of the Sentencing Guidelines and Information Committee *via* the Judicial Council Act 2019 may end up being the most significant statutory reform that impacts sentencing practice in the future.

Conclusion

This chapter highlighted the importance in examining the role and impact of judges on sentencing decisions at both trial and appellate level. The analysis revealed that these decisions are the product of a small group of judges that frequently make sexual offence sentencing decisions. This contributes to an understanding of the consistency evident in this specific group of cases. Judges employed their professional experiences as a means of gauging offence seriousness. There was evidence that sentencing remarks had a personal impact, with judges voicing difficulties in articulating the details of the offending in their remarks. The analysis of the appellate process showed that there are a multitude of impacts and influences emanating from the presence and practice of judicial oversight. This serves to underscore the importance of looking beyond aggravating and mitigating factors to incorporate the panoply of influences within the orbit of sentencing judges. Having taken an expansive approach to factors informing sentencing outcomes, some concluding thoughts are presented in the final chapter.

SEVEN

Conclusion

This book demonstrated the benefit of widening the lens of analysis to encapsulate a range of influences, from the macro to the micro, that can build a better understanding of how and why judges decide to impose a particular sentence for a specific offence or offences. This helped situate decision-making in its structural and ecological context. Analysing a small group of cases at the apex of seriousness in the sexual offence category provided an opportunity to explore, interpret and extrapolate the meaning of the picture that emerged. Whether by design or happenstance, that picture was fairly consistent, at least in terms of the profile of facts and factors that resulted in sentences of 15 years to life imprisonment.

The examination of the offending itself and more traditional factors influencing sentencing outcomes (such as aggravating and mitigating factors) was important in understanding judicial perspectives on seriousness in sexual offence cases. The multiplicity of offending was a key driver of sentence outcomes in almost all of these cases. There is a tendency in official statistics, and many studies, to focus the analysis on the principal offence but this can clearly lead to misrepresentation given the volume of crimes committed in these cases.[1] Expanding the scope of inquiry can also yield information on additional drivers outside of the aggravating and mitigating factors developed through the 'sentencing canon'. For example, the prevalence of stranger relationships in cases where an adult was victimised raised questions regarding whether perceptions of seriousness are being impacted by wider cultural beliefs such as the 'real rape' myth. Without reliable comparative data on sentencing in sexual offence cases more generally, it can be difficult to draw any strong conclusions from this, but the concern is valid and it is certainly worthy of further scrutiny.

In child sexual abuse cases there was evidence of differential approaches to sentencing outcomes based on the gender of the victim and the intra- and extra-familial relationship between the victim and the perpetrator. Societal and legal evolutions on issues relating to child sexual abuse during the course of this study also had an impact on cases coming before the courts. This serves as a reminder that the sentencing caseload is shaped by whether victims choose to disclose (or not) and the decisions made by the police, prosecution and jury (if there is a trial) along the route towards a conviction. As such, these decision-makers are important gatekeepers that can funnel certain types of cases towards (or away from) the sentencing court. Complex as this may be, it is important to try to understand the influence of the wider social and cultural frameworks as well as the role of actors, decision-makers and institutional structures in contributing to sentencing outcomes.

The research also provided insight into the diverse range of factors that play an important part in understanding decision-making. While there is often a laser-like focus on the reasons given by the judge for the sentencing outcome, these decisions are in fact the culmination of a range of prior decisions, collaborations and inputs made by a whole host of criminal justice professionals and participants in the process. The small number of judges responsible for sentencing in these cases was an important component in shedding light on the issue of consistency. As sentencers that regularly deal with sexual offences, their knowledge base and 'practical wisdom' is higher than what might be expected of judges in other courts around the country. As one judge was responsible for almost half of these decisions, the ability of an individual to shape sentencing policy and practice through embedding factors in their decision-making is important to reflect upon. The judicial oversight provided by the appellate courts also plays a direct role in reviewing individual decision-making. Indeed, the prospect that there is a high likelihood that a sentencing decision will be reviewed by judicial colleagues may also inform the decision itself and the reasons articulated for it.

Undoubtedly, judges' decisions are guided by a 'sentencing canon' of appellate judgments that can assist in the exercise of their 'principled discretion'. The decision by the appellate courts to embark on the development of sentencing guidance for specific offences in 2014 is indicative of the judiciary's willingness to engage with the consistency project. Specific guidance for the offence of rape was only issued by the Supreme Court towards the end of the period covered in this study. But many of the factors detailed in the sentencing band for 15 years to life imprisonment were evident in the cases in this study dating as far back as 1985. Part of the explanation for this derives from the methodology used to generate sentencing guidance. Sentencing bands are created based on an analysis of previous cases and the sentencing factors articulated at trial level as well as in appellate judgments. The combination of these are used to determine and articulate a list of established factors that may result in the offending being categorised as falling within a certain sentencing band in future cases.

This methodology has its merits. It can reflect what is already happening, collating and affirming factors that should be considered when deliberating on a sentence. It can also have the unintended consequence of embedding patterns that may, at the very least, require some further thought. Take the prevalence of stranger rape in cases involving adult victims resulting in 15 years to life imprisonment. The factors developed by the Supreme Court in the guidance for this sentencing band are based largely on the cases in this study where the parties were strangers to each other. This pattern may become unintentionally embedded in the guidance judgment and examples provided by the appellate courts in that judgment. This then increases the likelihood that sentencing judges will follow this pattern in future cases. It may inadvertently result in the exclusion of other sexual offences of equal seriousness from this sentencing band because the offending was perpetrated by, for example, an intimate partner. This further reinforces the merits in adopting an approach that looks at the 'whole case story'.[2] Doing so can lead to more meaningful discussions on what *is* being taken into consideration, what *ought* to be taken into consideration and what *ought not* to be taken into consideration.

A further difficulty that emerges in adopting this approach is that guidance developed by an appellate court for a specific offence rarely reflects on penalty ranges, guidance and sentencing bands that apply to other offences with the same maximum penalty.[3] When creating offence-specific guidance, it is important to take account of the bigger picture such that the sentencing bands created through these guidance judgments can be justified internally (in relation to the specific offence) and externally (when reflecting on sentencing across a range of different offences).

In the pursuit of a sentencing elixir, some countries have adopted wide-ranging reforms, with many opting for the sentencing guidelines approach. In Ireland, with the establishment of the Sentencing Guidelines and Information Committee, it appears a similar trajectory is on the horizon. This situation has been made somewhat unclear by a recent Supreme Court decision that examined the guidelines created by another body (the Personal Injuries Guidelines Committee) that raises some question regarding the compatibility of future sentencing guidelines with *Bunreacht na hÉireann* (the Irish Constitution).[4] Irrespective of this, given that the movement towards guidelines is still in its early stages, Ireland has an opportunity to paddle its own canoe, once again. Taking the time to generate rich, layered and nuanced data on sentencing may prove fruitful in navigating the course ahead. It is hoped that this book may serve as an example of the benefits in taking a broad approach when exploring the complexities of sentencing decision-making.

Notes

one

1 Tata, C. (2020) *Sentencing: A Social Process.* Cham: Palgrave Macmillan, p 2.

2 Central Statistics Office (2023) *Sexual Violence Survey 2022 – Main Results.* Dublin: Central Statistics Office.

3 Hanly, C., Healy, D. and Scriver, S. (2009) *Rape & Justice in Ireland: A National Study of Survivor, Prosecutor and Court Responses to Rape.* Dublin: The Liffey Press.

4 Central Statistics Office (2024) *Recorded Crime Detention 2023.* Dublin: Central Statistics Office.

5 Temkin, J. and Krahé, B. (2008) *Sexual Assault and the Justice Gap: A Question of Attitude* (1st ed). Oxford: Hart.

6 *DPP v J McD* [2021] IECA 31 [2021] 2 JIC 0802.

7 Prison Service (2008–2024) *Annual Reports.* Dublin and Longford: Irish Prison Service. Ireland does not record sentence committals of 15 years or more as a specific data category.

8 Aebi, M.F., Cocco, E. and Molnar, L. (2023) *SPACE I – Annual Penal Statistics: Prison Populations 2022.* Strasbourg: Council of Europe and University of Lausanne, p 52.

9 Tonry, M. (2007) 'Determinants of penal policies', *Crime and Justice, 36*(1): 1–48.

10 Aas, K.F. (2012) ' "The Earth is one but the world is not": Criminological theory and its geopolitical divisions', *Theoretical Criminology, 16*(1): 5–20.

11 O'Malley, T. (2016) *Sentencing Law and Practice* (3rd ed). Dublin: Thomson Round Hall, p 1.

12 Tata (2020), p 28.

13 Freiberg, A. and Roberts, J.V. (2023) 'March. Sentencing commissions and guidelines: A case study in policy transfer', *Criminal Law Forum, 34*(1): 87–129.

14 Tata (2020), p 15.

15 Brown, G. (2017) *Criminal Sentencing as Practical Wisdom.* Oxford: Hart Publishing.

16 Tata (2020), p 27.

17 *DPP v FE* [2019] IESC 85 [2020] 1 ILRM 517.

18 Griffin, D. (2018) *Killing Time: Life Imprisonment and Parole in Ireland.* Cham: Palgrave Macmillan, p 55.

19 United Nations Centre for Social Development and Humanitarian Affairs Crime Prevention and Criminal Justice Branch (1994) *Life Imprisonment.* Vienna: United Nations.

20 *DPP v S. (P.)* [2009] IECCA 1.

21 Griffin (2018).

22 Ashworth, A. and Wasik, M. (2018) 'Sentencing the multiple offender: In search of a "just and proportionate" sentence', in J. Ryberg, J.V. Roberts and J.W. De Keijser (eds) *Sentencing Multiple Crimes.* Oxford: Oxford University Press, p 211.

23 *Irish Times*, 'Life terms for rape, sex assault' (published 30 July 1999).

24 Estrich, S. (1987) *Real Rape: How the Legal System Victimizes Women Who Say No.* Cambridge, MA: Harvard University Press.

25 Hanly et al (2009); Möller, A.S., Bäckström, T., Söndergaard, H.P. and Helström, L. (2012) 'Patterns of injury and reported violence depending on relationship to assailant in female Swedish sexual assault victims', *Journal of Interpersonal Violence*, *27*(16): 3131–3148.

26 Wieberneit, M., Thal, S., Clare, J., Notebaert, L. and Tubex, H. (2024) 'Silenced survivors: A systematic review of the barriers to reporting, investigating, prosecuting, and sentencing of adult female rape and sexual assault', *Trauma, Violence, & Abuse*, *25*(5): 3742–3757.

27 Ring, S., Gleeson, K. and Stevenson, K. (2022) *Child Sexual Abuse Reported by Adult Survivors: Legal Responses in England and Wales, Ireland and Australia.* London: Routledge, p 152.

28 Hogan, G. and Whyte, G. (2004) *The Irish Constitution* (4th ed). Dublin: Butterworths.

29 O'Toole, M. (2024) *Report of the Scoping Inquiry into Historical Sexual Abuse in Day and Boarding Schools Run by Religious Orders.* Dublin: Education Scoping Inquiry.

30 Healy, D. and Griffin, D. (2023) 'Unnesting the matryoshka doll: An ecological model of probation and parole decision-making in Ireland', *Journal of Contemporary Criminal Justice*, *39*(1): 75–93; Rubin, A.T. and Phelps, M.S. (2017) 'Fracturing the penal state: State actors and the role of conflict in penal change', *Theoretical Criminology*, *21*(4): 422–440.

31 Courts Service (2024) *Annual Report.* Dublin: Courts Service, p 108.

32 O'Malley, T. (2001) 'Principled discretion: Towards the development of a sentencing canon', *The Bar Review*, *7*(3): 135–139.

33 Brown (2017).

34 *DPP v O'Brien* [2018] IECA 2, para 35.

35 McLean, S. and Cunningham, G. (2010) 'A man was yesterday given five life sentences for the rape and assault of a woman, one of the harshest sentences for rape handed down in an Irish court', *Irish Independent* (Dublin, 30 January 2010).

36 *Irish Times*, 'Dundalk man gets 20 years for incest' (published 15 January 1994).

37 *Irish Times*, 'Man who treated cleaner as a slave and "sex object" jailed for 15 years' (published 31 October 2019).

38 *Irish Times*, '36-year sentence for brother who sexually abused boys for years' (published 24 November 1999).

39 *Irish Times*, 'Father jailed for abuse and rape of three daughters over 18-year period' (published 19 May 2015).

two

1 O'Malley, T. (2001) 'Principled discretion: Towards the development of a sentencing canon', *The Bar Review*, *7*(3): 135–139; O'Malley, T. (2011) *Sentencing: Towards a Coherent System*. Dublin: Round Hall.

2 *DPP v Tiernan* [1989] ILRM 149 p 250.

3 O'Malley, T. (2003) 'Sentencing values and sentencing structures', *Judicial Studies Institute Journal*, *3*(1): 130–147, 147.

4 O'Malley, T. (2014) 'A quiet revolution occurred this month: Sentencing guidelines were introduced: Consistency in sentencing is sensible, provided there is flexibility to cater for exceptional cases', *Irish Times* (Dublin, 31 March 2014).

5 Wasik, M. (2003) 'Sentencing guidelines: past, present, and future', *Current Legal Problems*, *56*(1): 239–264.

6 *Irish Times*, 'Judge calls rape bestial and gives men 21 years' (Dublin, 9 October 1985); *Irish Times*, 'Court refuses to reduce rape jail term' (Dublin, 14 January 1986).

7 *DPP v Tiernan* [1989] ILRM 149, p 250.

8 *Irish Times*, 'Court refuses to reduce rape jail term' (Dublin, 14 January 1986).

9 This was enabled by the Attorney General, who certified that the case involved a point of law of exceptional public importance. It was in the public interest, according to the Attorney General, that the Supreme Court produce a decision on 'the guidelines which the courts should apply in relation to sentences for the crime of rape'. *DPP v Tiernan* [1989] ILRM 149, p 251.

10 *DPP v Tiernan* [1989] ILRM 149, p 254.

11 O'Malley, T. (2016) *Sentencing Law and Practice* (3rd ed). Dublin: Thomson Round Hall, p 796.

12 O'Malley (2016), p 772.

13 *DPP v K (D)* [2002] 3 IR 534.

14 Maguire, N. and Carr, N. (2017) *Probation Service Research Report: Individualising Justice: Pre-sentence Reports in the Irish Criminal Justice System*. Dublin: The Probation Service, p 26.

15 s.5 Criminal Justice Act 1993 as amended by the Criminal Procedure Act 2010.

16 Hanly, C., Healy, D. and Scriver, S. (2009) *Rape & Justice in Ireland: A National Study of Survivor, Prosecutor and Court Responses to Rape*. Dublin: The Liffey Press, p 349.

17 O'Malley, T. (2006) *Sentencing Law and Practice* (2nd ed). Dublin: Thomson Round Hall, p 591.

18 *DPP v J McD* [2021] IECA 31 [2021] 2 JIC 0802, para 52.

19 *DPP v M* [1994] 3 IR 306.

20 *DPP v M* [1994] 3 IR 306.

21 O'Malley (2001).

22 Brown, G. (2020) *Sentencing Rape: A Comparative Analysis*. Oxford: Bloomsbury Publishing, p 165.

23 *DPP v J McD* [2021] IECA 31 [2021] 2 JIC 0802.

24 *DPP v O'Brien* [2018] IECA 2, para 35.

25 Browne, G. (2017) *Criminal Sentencing as Practical Wisdom*. Hart: Oxford; O'Malley (2001); (2011).

26 *DPP v O'Brien* [2018] IECA 2, para 45.

27 *DPP v SC* [2019] IECA 348.

28 *DPP v O'Brien* [2018] IECA 2, para 46.

29 *DPP v McGinley*, Court of Criminal Appeal, 12 July 2011; *Irish Times*, 'Appeal against conviction for raping woman (85) fails' (published 12 July 2011).

30 *DPP v Conroy (No.2)* [1989] IR 160.

31 *DPP v X* [2021] IECA 168, para 101; *DPP v ET* [2016] IECA 312, paras 19–25; *DPP v Cummins* [2008] IECA 92.

32 *DPP v Cooney* [2004] unreported, Court of Criminal Appeal, 27 July 2004.

33 O'Malley, T. (2009) *The Criminal Process*. Dublin: Thomas Reuters, p 877; *DPP v R McC and CD* [2007] IESC 47 [2008] 2 IR 92, 104.

34 O'Malley (2009), p 876.

35 *DPP v O'Brien* [2018] IECA 2, para 35.

36 *DPP v Molloy* [2016] IECA 239.

37 *DPP v Molloy* [2016] IECA 239; *DPP v O'Brien* [2018] IECA 2, para 35.

38 s.2 Criminal Law (Rape) Act 1981, as amended by s.21 of the Criminal Law (Rape) (Amendment) Act 1990.

39 s.4 Criminal Law (Rape) (Amendment) Act 1990.

40 s.3 Criminal Law (Rape) (Amendment) Act 1990.

41 s.2 Criminal Law (Sexual Offences) Act 2006. In s.3 of the Act it is an offence to engage in a sexual act with a child under the age

of 17. If that person is a person in authority the maximum sentence is 15 years' imprisonment.

42 Trafficking of children for the purpose of sexual exploitation also has a maximum penalty of life imprisonment, however as this is a trafficking offence it has been excluded from the analysis. s.3(1)(b) Child Trafficking and Pornography Act 1998, as amended by s.3 of Criminal Law (Human Trafficking) Act 1998 (amended by s.6 Criminal Law (Sexual Offences) (Amendment) Act 2007).

43 s.12 Criminal Justice Act 1993; s.5 Criminal Law (Incest Proceedings) Act 1995.

44 s.21 Criminal Law (Sexual Offences) Act 2017; Protected person is defined as a person that lacks the capacity to consent to a sexual act because of mental or intellectual disability or a mental illness. This offence replaced an offence that focused on mental impairment created in 1993 that had a maximum penalty of 10 years imprisonment.

45 s.2 Criminal Law (Rape) Act 1981.

46 s.3(1) Criminal Law (Rape) (Amendment) Act 1990.

47 s.3 Criminal Law (Sexual Offences) Act 2017; in addition, offences committed by persons in authority with a child under the age of 17 carries a maximum penalty of 15 years' imprisonment since 2017, an increase from seven years previously (s.3 Criminal Law (Sexual Offences) Act 2017).

48 See: Criminal Law Amendment Act 1935; Doyle, D.M. (2012) 'Reasonable Belief and Unlawful Carnal Knowledge: A Historical Perspective', *Irish Jurist*, *47*: 49–75.

49 O'Malley (2016), p 1.

50 For example: *DPP v Meyer Hustveit* [2016] IECA 271 [2016] 3 JIC 1512. In this case a suspended sentence was appealed based on 'undue leniency' and was then increased to 15 months.

51 *DPP v FE* [2019] IESC 85 [2020] 1 ILRM 517.

52 Courts Service (2022) *Annual Report*, Dublin: Courts Service, p 108.

53 Freiberg, A. and Roberts, J.V. (2023) 'March: Sentencing Commissions and Guidelines: A Case Study in Policy Transfer', *Criminal Law Forum*, *34*(1): 87–129, Dordrecht: Springer Netherlands, p 88.

54 Freiberg and Roberts (2023), p 125.

55 Tonry, M. (1996) *Sentencing Matters*. New York: Oxford University Press.

56 Stith, K. and Cabranes, J. (1998) *Fear of Judging: Sentencing Guidelines in the Federal Courts*. Chicago: Chicago University Press.

57 Freiberg and Roberts (2023), p 125.

58 Sentencing Council of England and Wales (2013) *Sexual Offences Definitive Guideline*. London: Sentencing Council of England and Wales.

59 Roberts, J.V. (2019) 'The evolution of sentencing guidelines in Minnesota and England and Wales', *Crime and Justice*, *48*(1): 187–253; Ashworth, A.

and Padfield, N. (2015) 'Editorial – Five years of the Sentencing Council', *Criminal Law Review*, 657–658.

60 *R v Thelwall* [2016] EWCA Crim 1755.

61 Pina-Sánchez, J., Gosling, J.P., Chung, H.I., Bourgeois, E., Geneletti, S., and Marder, I.D. (2019) 'Have the England and Wales guidelines affected sentencing severity? An empirical analysis using a scale of severity and time-series analyses', *The British Journal of Criminology*, *59*(4): 979–1001.

62 Howard League for Penal Reform (2024) *Sentencing Inflation: A Judicial Critique*. London: Howard League for Penal Reform. The conviction in this case was quashed and a retrial ordered by the Court of Criminal Appeal based on the judge's directions to the jury during the trial. *DPP v WD* [2008] IECCA 91.

63 *DPP v WD* [2008] 1 IR 308.

64 *DPP v Keane* [2008] 3 IR 177.

65 Conroy, B. and Gunning, P. (2009) 'The Irish sentencing information system (ISIS): A practical guide to a practical tool', *Judicial Studies Institute Journal*, *1*: 37–53; O'Cathaoir, K. (2012) *Recent Rape Sentencing Analysis: The WD Case & Beyond*. Dublin: Judicial Researchers Office. [No longer publicly available.]

66 s.23 Judicial Council Act 2019.

67 Gormley, J., O'Malley, T., Roberts, J., Spohn, C. and Tata, C. (2023) *Assessing Methodological Approaches to Sentencing Data and Analysis*. Dublin: Sentencing Guidelines and Information Committee.

68 O'Malley (2014).

69 *DPP v Ryan* [2014] IECCA 11.

70 *DPP v Fitzgibbon* [2014] ILRM 116.

71 *DPP v Ryan* [2014] IECCA 11.

72 *DPP v Ryan* [2014] IECCA 11.

73 *DPP v Mahon* [2019] IESC 24.

74 *DPP v O'Sullivan* [2020] 11 JIC 2601.

75 O'Malley T. (2023) 'Annual distinguished lecture 2023: From practical wisdom to guidelines: The future of sentencing regulation', Galway: University of Galway (11 May 2023).

76 *DPP v J McD* [2021] IECA 31 [2021] 2 JIC 0802.

77 *DPP v F.E.* [2019] IESC 85 [2020] 1 ILRM 517.

78 *DPP v J McD* [2021] IECA 31 [2021] 2 JIC 0802.

79 Gormley et al (2023).

80 *DPP v Ryan* [2014] IECCA 11.

three

1 In the rare instances where there were co-defendants and these co-defendants were each sentenced to 15 years or more, each defendant was counted as an individual case.

2 Accessed through subscriber-based and freely available legal databases Westlaw, Lexis, Justis etc.

3 Accessed through newspaper archives *via* ProQuest.

4 Cases where a defendant successfully appealed on an issue relating to the conviction were excluded from the study as the impact of a successful appeal against conviction invalidates the sentence also. Cases where an appeal against sentence resulted in a reduction in sentence were included in this study as the focus is on the sentencing judge's assessment of seriousness. In addition, assessments of seriousness by sentencing judges were overwhelmingly approved of on appeal irrespective of whether the sentence was reduced or not (see Chapter 6).

5 Tata, C. (2020) *Sentencing: A Social Process*. Cham: Palgrave Macmillan, p 40.

6 Tata (2020), p 43.

7 Steffensmeier, D., Ulmer, J. and Kramer, J. (1998) 'The interaction of race, gender, and age in criminal sentencing: The punishment cost of being young, black, and male', *Criminology*, *36*(4): 763–798.

8 Steffensmeier et al (1998).

9 Engen, R.L. and Gainey, R.R. (2000) 'Modeling the effects of legally relevant and extralegal factors under sentencing guidelines: The rules have changed', *Criminology*, *38*(4): 1207–1230; Pina-Sánchez, J. and Linacre, R. (2013) 'Sentence consistency in England and Wales: Evidence from the Crown Court sentencing survey', *British Journal of Criminology*, *53*(6): 1118–1138.

10 O'Malley, T. (2017) 'Judgment and calculation in the selection of sentence', *Criminal Law Forum*, *28*: 361–389.

11 s.6(1) of the Criminal Law (Rape) Act 1981, as amended by s.11 of the Criminal Law (Rape) (Amendment) Act 1990.

12 Hanly, C., Healy, D. and Scriver, S. (2009) *Rape & Justice in Ireland: A National Study of Survivor, Prosecutor and Court Responses to Rape*. Dublin: The Liffey Press; Corr, M., O'Mahony, P., Lovett, J. and Kelly, L. (2009) *Different Systems, Similar Outcomes? Tracking Attrition in Reported Rape Cases in Eleven Countries (country briefing: Ireland)*. London: Child and Woman Abuse Studies Unit.

13 O'Malley, T. (2013) *Sexual Offences* (2nd ed). Dublin: Round Hall, Chapters 25 and 26.

14 O'Cathaoir, K. (2012) *Recent Rape Sentencing Analysis: The WD Case & Beyond*. Dublin: Judicial Researchers Office. [No longer publicly available.]

15 Jewkes, M. (2004) 'Media representations of the causes of crime', *Criminal Justice Matters*, *55*(1): 26–27.

16 O'Connell, M. (1999) 'Is Irish public opinion towards crime distorted by media bias?', *European Journal of Communication*, *14*(2): 191–212.

17 Healy, D. and O'Donnell, I. (2010) 'Crime, consequences and court reports', *Irish Criminal Law Journal*, *20*(1): 2–7.

18 Tata, C. (2007) 'Sentencing as craftwork and the binary epistemologies of the discretionary decision process', *Social & Legal Studies*, *16*(3): 425–447.

19 102 of 108 cases.

20 Ryberg, J., Roberts, J.V. and De Keijser, J.W. (eds) (2018) *Sentencing Multiple Crimes*. Oxford: Oxford University Press, p 2.

21 Ashworth, A. and Wasik, M. (2018) 'Sentencing the Multiple Offender: In search of a "just and proportionate" sentence', in J. Ryberg, J.V. Roberts and J.W. De Keijser (eds) *Sentencing Multiple Crimes*. Oxford: Oxford University Press, p 211.

22 Office of the Director of Public Prosecutions (2019) *Guidelines for Prosecutors* (5th ed). Dublin: Office of the Director of Public Prosecutions, p 22.

23 *DPP v AD* [2018] IECA 308; *DPP v Casey* [2018] IECA 121.

24 Griffin, D. (2018) *Killing Time: Life Imprisonment and Parole in Ireland*. Cham: Palgrave Macmillan, p 5.

25 *DPP v Casey* [2018] IECA 121. Sentencing judges may also select the most serious offence arising from a single incident and calculate a global headline sentence that represents the totality of the offending. This offence is referred to as the 'gauge offence'. The other offences are taken into consideration when calculating this sentence. This is not considered best practice. *DPP v Jones* [2021], unreported, Court of Appeal, 21 November 2021.

26 88 of 102 cases. It was not possible to identify if concurrent or consecutive sentences were imposed in two cases although there is a presumption that cases run concurrently when there is a lack of clarity. O'Malley, T. (2006) *Sentencing Law and Practice* (2nd ed). Dublin: Thomson Round Hall, p 200.

27 *DPP v SC* [2019] IECA 348.

28 O'Malley, T. (2016) *Sentencing Law and Practice* (3rd ed). Dublin: Thomson Round Hall, p 111.

29 *DPP v FE* [2019] IESC 85 [2019] 1 ILRM 517; *DPP v SC* [2019] IECA 348.

30 *DPP v PP* [2019] IECA 246.

31 *DPP v KC* [2019] IECA 126.

32 Ashworth and Wasik (2018), p 211.

33 *DPP v Farrell* [2010] IECCA 68.

34 *Gilligan v Ireland and ors* [2014] 1 ILRM 153.

35 *DPP v SC* [2019] IECA 348.

36 *DPP v SC* [2019] IECA 348.

37 *DPP v PP* [2019] IECA 246.

38 van Zyl Smit, D. and Appleton, C. (2019) *Life Imprisonment: A Global Human Rights Analysis*. Harvard: Harvard University Press, p 71.

39 *DPP v Mahon* [2019] IESC 24.

40 *Irish Times*, 'Double sex-killer gets 18-year jail sentence' (Dublin, 27 July 1996); *DPP v Piotrowski* [2014] IECCA 41 [2014] 11 JIC 2704.

41 Griffin, D. (2020) 'Life imprisonment and the Parole Act 2019: Assessing the potential impact on parole decision-making', *Irish Judicial Studies Journal*, *4*(1): 24–44.

42 Sheleff, L. (1987) *Ultimate Penalties: Capital Punishment, Life Imprisonment, Physical Torture*. Columbus: Ohio State University Press.

43 Ghandnoosh, N. (2017) *Delaying a Second Chance: The Declining Prospects for Parole on Life Sentences*. Washington, DC: Sentencing Project.

44 O'Malley (2016), p 649.

45 45 of 86 cases. Life sentence cases were excluded here as it is not possible to part-suspend a sentence of life imprisonment.

46 *Re McIlhagga*, unreported, Supreme Court, 29 July 1971; s.99 Criminal Justice Act 2006.

47 s.99 Criminal Justice Act 2006.

48 Courts Service (2024) *Annual Report*. Dublin: Courts Service, p 108.

49 Sex Offenders Act 2001, Parts 2, 3 and 5 as amended by the Sex Offenders (Amendment) Act 2001; O'Malley (2016), pp 397–406.

50 Sex Offenders Act 2001, Part 2.

51 25 of 65 cases. Post-release supervision orders are not ordinarily applied to those serving life imprisonment as they are released via the parole process and they remain under supervision for the rest of their lives on release.

52 O'Malley, T. (2003) 'Sentencing values and sentencing structures', *Judicial Studies Institute Journal*, *3*(1): 130–147, p 134.

53 Rule 59, Prison Rules 2007: S.I. No 252 of 2007; Joint Committee on Justice, Defence and Equality (2013) *Report on Penal Reform*. Dublin: Stationery Office, p 15.

54 *O'Brien v Minister for Justice and Prison Service* [2017] IEHC 199.

55 *O'Brien v Minister for Justice and Prison Service* [2017] IEHC 199.

56 s.2 Criminal Justice Act 1960.

57 Department of Justice, Equality and Law Reform (2009) *The Management of Sex Offenders: A Discussion Document*. Dublin: Department of Justice and Law Reform, p 48.

58 van Zyl Smit and Appleton (2019), pp 142, 381.

59 Griffin, D. (2024) '"Dangerous" and "Devious": Exploring judicial rationales when imposing a discretionary sentence of life imprisonment', *Irish Judicial Studies Journal*, *8*(1): 1–18.

60 Griffin (2024).

61 *DPP v McC and CD* [2007] IESC 47, [2008] 1 ILRM 321.

62 *DPP v Z* [2014] IECCA 13, [2014] 2 ILRM 132.

63 s.24(1)(a) Parole Act 2019. Griffin, D. (2015) 'The release and recall of life sentence prisoners: Policy, practice and politics', *Irish Jurist*, *53*: 1–35.

64 Griffin (2018), p10.

65 Griffin (2018), p 5.

66 *DPP v Mahon* [2019] IESC 24.

67 s.27, Parole Act 2019.

68 *Irish Times*, 'Rapist is sentenced to penal servitude for life' (Dublin, 1 July 1992).

69 *DPP v Duffy* [2009] unreported, Court of Criminal Appeal, 19 January 2009.

70 *Irish Times*, 'Judge says life sentence not open' (Dublin, 25 January 1997).

71 *DPP v PS* [2009] IECCA 1.

72 *Irish Times*, Ronan McGreevy, 'Riedo Killer given life for rape' (Dublin, 24 July 2009).

73 *Irish Times*, 'Escaped serial offender gets life for rape' (Dublin, 11 June 2009).

74 *DPP v G* [1994] 1 IR 587.

75 *DPP v Egan* [2017] IECA 95; *DPP v McC and CD* [2008] 1 ILRM 321.

76 Griffin (2018), p 18.

77 Griffin, D. and Healy, D. (2019) 'The pains of parole for life sentence prisoners in Ireland: Risk, rehabilitation and re-entry', *European Journal of Probation*, *11*(3): 124–138.

78 O'Malley (2016), p 85.

79 *Lynch and Whelan v Minister for Justice* [2012] 1 IR 1; Griffin, D. and O'Donnell, I. (2016) 'Confusingly compliant with the European Convention on Human Rights: The Release of Life Sentence Prisoners in Ireland', in D. van Zyl Smit and C. Appleton (eds) *Life Imprisonment and Human Rights*. Oxford: Hart Publishing, pp 267–288.

80 *DPP v MS* [2000] 2 I.R. 592 at pp 600 and 601; *DPP v Daniels* [2015] 1 I.L.R.M. 99.

81 *DPP v Daniels* [2014] IESC 64 para 21; *DPP v Jackson* [1993] IECA, 26 April; *DPP v Egan* [2017] IECA 95.

four

1 39 cases – in three cases it was not possible to identify offence seriousness remarks.

2 *DPP v Murray* [2017] IECA 292, para 15.

3 *Irish Times*, 'Man is jailed for 17 years for rape of two Australian women' (Dublin, 22 February 2003).

4 *Irish Times*, 'Teen rapist sentenced to 15 years penal servitude' (Dublin, 21 December 1994).

5 *Irish Times*, 'A man was yesterday given five life sentences for the rape and assault of a woman, one of the harshest sentences for rape handed down in an Irish court' (Dublin, 30 January 2010).

6 *Irish Examiner*, '15 year jail term for "social deviant" who raped aunt' (Dublin, 29 July 2011).
7 *Irish Times*, 'Man gets 15 years for rape of his mother' (Dublin, 2 October 2012).
8 *Irish Times*, 'Judge calls rape bestial and gives men 21 years' (Dublin, 9 October 1985).
9 *Selim v Governor of Midlands Prison* [2017] IEHC 292 [2017] 6 SSP; *Irish Independent*, 'Rapist gets 16 years for 'barbaric' sex assault' (Dublin, 27 April 2006).
10 *DPP v FE* [2019] IESC 85 [2020] 1 ILRM 517.
11 *DPP v FE* [2019] IESC 85 [2020] 1 ILRM 517.
12 It not always possible to identify a location and so there are likely additional locations where offending took place.
13 O'Malley, T. (2016) *Sentencing Law and Practice* (3rd ed). Dublin: Thomson Round Hall, p 655.
14 *DPP v FE* [2019] IESC 85 [2020] 1 ILRM 517.
15 *Irish Times*, 'Man gets 21 years for raping woman (86)' (Dublin, 16 July 2009).
16 O'Malley (2016), p 159; Padfield, N. and Roberts, J.V. (2011) 'Intoxication as a sentencing factor: Mitigation or aggravation', in J.V. Roberts (ed) *Mitigation and Aggravating at Sentencing*. Cambridge: Cambridge University Press, pp 81–101.
17 O'Malley (2016), p 159.
18 *Irish Times*, 'Man gets 21 years for raping woman (86)' (Dublin, 16 July 2009).
19 *DPP v WD* [2007] IEHC 310; *DPP v FE* [2019] IESC 85, para 57 [2020] 1 ILRM 517.
20 *DPP v Gierlowski* [2021] IECA 13.
21 *DPP v Gierlowski* [2021] IECA 13.
22 *Irish Times*, 'Man gets 21 years for raping woman (86)' (Dublin, 16 July 2009).
23 *Selim v Governor of Midlands Prison* [2017] IEHC 292 [2017] 6 SSP.
24 *DPP v Goidan* [2022] IECA 202.
25 *Irish Times*, 'Father of two gets 15 years for rape of Spanish au pair' (Dublin, 15 February 2006).
26 *DPP v K.(G.)* [2008] IECCA 110.
27 *Irish Examiner*, 'Dublin man given 20 years for raping two women' (Dublin, 15 May 2009).
28 *Irish Independent*, 'Repeat rapist to appeal length of sentence' (Dublin, 17 February 2009).
29 O'Malley, T. (2006) *Sentencing Law and Practice* (2nd ed). Dublin: Thomson Round Hall, p 92.

30 Brown, G. (2020) *Sentencing Rape: A Comparative Analysis*. Oxford: Bloomsbury Publishing, p 46.

31 *Irish Examiner*, 'Dublin man given 20 years for raping two women' (Dublin, 15 May 2009).

32 *Irish Times*, 'Man given 15 years for rape in public toilets' (Dublin, 29 June 2011).

33 *Irish Times*, 'Man gets 21 years for raping woman (86)' (Dublin, 16 July 2009).

34 *Irish Times*, 'Man jailed for 18 years for rape and assault' (Dublin, 24 April 2018).

35 s.5 Criminal Justice Act 1993 as amended by the Criminal Procedure Act 2010.

36 s.31 Criminal Justice (Victims of Crime) Act 2017.

37 s.5 Criminal Justice Act 1993 as substituted by s.4 Criminal Procedure Act 2010.

38 This includes instances of evidence given by the victim that arose in cases prior to victim impact statements being placed on a statutory footing.

39 *Irish Times*, 'Man jailed for 17 years for rape of two Australian women' (Dublin, 22 February 2003).

40 *Irish Times*, 'Man who treated cleaner as a slave and "sex object" jailed for 15 years' (Dublin, 31 October 2019).

41 *DPP v McKeon* [2021] IECA 212.

42 *Irish Times*, 'Multiple rapist is jailed for 18 years' (Dublin, 18 October 1996).

43 *Irish Examiner*, 'Dublin man given 20 years for raping two women' (Dublin, 15 May 2009).

44 Roberts, J.V. and Erez, E. (2004) 'Communication in sentencing: Exploring the expressive function of victim impact statements', *International Review of Victimology*, *10*(3): 223–244; Cassell, P.G. (2008) 'In defense of victim impact statements', *Ohio State Journal of Criminal Law*, *6*, 611; Guiry, R. (2006) 'Who is the Victim? The Use of Victim Impact Statements in Murder and Manslaughter cases', *Irish Criminal Law Journal*, *6*(3): 2.

45 *DPP v WD* [2008] 1 IR 308.

46 Roberts, J.V. (1997) 'The role of criminal record in the sentencing process', *Crime and Justice*, *22*: 303–362.

47 Borum, R., Swartz, M. and Swanson, J. (1996) 'Assessing and managing violence risk in clinical practice', *Journal of Psychiatric Practice*, *2*(4): 205–215.

48 *DPP v K.(G.)* [2008] IECCA 110.

49 *DPP v K.(G.)* [2008] IECCA 110.

50 s.4 Criminal Law (Sexual Offences) (Amendment) Act 2019.

51 Previous criminal history was not identifiable in the remaining four cases (8.9 per cent).

52 *Irish Times*, 'Man given 15 years for rape in public toilets' (Dublin, 29 June 2011).
53 *Irish Times*, 'Man gets 21 years for raping woman (86)' (Dublin, 16 July 2009).
54 s.10 Bail Act 1997.
55 Maguire, N. and Carr, N. (2017) *Probation Service Research Report: Individualising Justice: Pre-sentence Reports in the Irish Criminal Justice System*. Dublin: The Probation Service, p 26.
56 *Irish Times*, 'Teenage rapist sentenced to 15 years penal servitude' (Dublin, 21 December 1994).
57 *Irish Times*, 'Man jailed for 20 years for rape and robbery' (Dublin, 12 February 1987).
58 *Irish Times*, 'Man jailed for 20 years for rape and robbery' (Dublin, 12 February 1987).
59 McGreevy, R., 'Riedo killer given two life terms for raping student', *Irish Times* (Dublin, 25 July 2009).
60 *Irish Times*, 'Rapist who attacked a grandmother "needs to be removed from society"' (Dublin, 13 December 2016).
61 *DPP v Cummins* [2008] IECA 92.
62 *Irish Times*, 'Nenagh man jailed for 15 years for raping widow (75)' (Dublin, 13 March 2007).
63 In four cases (or 8.8 per cent) the offender pleaded guilty to some but not all offences.
64 In four cases (or 16 per cent) it was not possible to identify at what point the guilty plea was entered.
65 *DPP v Molloy* [2016] IECA 239.
66 *DPP v Ward* [2012] IECCA 15, [2012] 1 JIC 1601.
67 *DPP v McKeon* [2021] IECA 212.
68 *Irish Times*, '15 years for rape, kidnapping and murder attempt' (Dublin, 12 May 2001).
69 *DPP v K.(G.)* [2008] IECCA 110.
70 *DPP v Z* [2014] 2 ILRM 132.
71 In ten cases it was not possible to identify mitigating factors.
72 *Irish Times*, 'Man gets 21 years for raping woman (86)' (Dublin, 16 July 2009).
73 *Irish Times*, '"Social deviant" who raped aunt jailed for 15 years' (Dublin, 30 July 2011).
74 Estrich, S. (1987) *Real Rape: How the Legal System Victimizes Women Who Say No*. Cambridge, MA: Harvard University Press.
75 Ellison, L. and Munro, V.E. (2010) 'A stranger in the bushes, or an elephant in the room? Critical reflections upon received rape myth wisdom in the context of a mock jury study', *New Criminal Law Review*, *13*(4): 781–801; McGee, H., Garavan, R., de Barra, M., Byrne, J. and Conroy, R. (2002)

The SAVI Report: Sexual Abuse and Victimization in Ireland. Dublin: The Liffey Press.

76 Christie, N. (1986) 'The ideal victim', in E.A. Fattah (ed) *From Crime Policy to Victim Policy: Reorienting the Justice System*. London: Palgrave Macmillan UK, pp 17–30.

77 Ellison and Munro (2010); Temkin, J. and Krahé, B. (2008) *Sexual Assault and the Justice Gap: A Question of Attitude* (1st ed). Oxford: Hart.

78 Central Statistics Office (2023) *Sexual Violence Survey 2022 – Main Results*. Dublin: Central Statistics Office.

79 Ministry of Justice, Home Office and the Office for National Statistics (2013) *An Overview of Sexual Offending in England and Wales – Statistics Bulletin*, London, Ministry of Justice, Home Office and the Office for National Statistics; Jones, J.S., Wynn, B.N., Kroeze, B., Dunnuck, C. and Rossman, L. (2004) 'Comparison of sexual assaults by strangers versus known assailants in a community-based population', *The American Journal of Emergency Medicine*, *22*(6): 454–459.

80 Central Statistics Office (2023); Hanly, C., Healy, D. and Scriver, S. (2009) *Rape & Justice in Ireland: A National Study of Survivor, Prosecutor and Court Responses to Rape*. Dublin: The Liffey Press; Corr, M., O'Mahony, P., Lovett, J. and Kelly, L. (2009) *Different Systems, Similar Outcomes? Tracking Attrition in Reported Rape Cases in Eleven Countries (country briefing: Ireland)*. London: Child and Woman Abuse Studies Unit; Leahy, S. (2014) 'Bad laws or bad attitudes? Assessing the impact of societal attitudes upon the conviction rate for rape in Ireland', *Irish Journal of Applied Social Studies*, *14*(1): 18–29.

81 Hanly et al (2009), p 268.

82 Central Statistics Office (2023).

83 Wieberneit, M., Thal, S., Clare, J., Notebaert, L. and Tubex, H. (2024) 'Silenced survivors: A systematic review of the barriers to reporting, investigating, prosecuting, and sentencing of adult female rape and sexual assault', *Trauma, Violence, & Abuse*, *25*(5): 3742–3757.

84 Möller, A.S., Bäckström, T., Söndergaard, H.P. and Helström, L. (2012) 'Patterns of injury and reported violence depending on relationship to assailant in female Swedish sexual assault victims', *Journal of Interpersonal Violence*, *27*(16): 3131–3148.

85 Möller et al (2012); McCall-Hosenfeld, J.S., Freund, K.M. and Liebschutz, J.M. (2009) 'Factors associated with sexual assault and time to presentation', *Preventive Medicine*, *48*(6): 593–595; Stermac, L., Bove, G.D. and Addison, M. (2001) 'Violence, injury, and presentation patterns in spousal sexual assaults', *Violence Against Women*, *7*(11): 1218–1233.

86 s.40 Domestic Violence Act 2018.

87 Sentencing Guidelines Council (2007) *Sexual Offences Act 2003 – Definitive Guidelines*. London: Sentencing Guidelines Council; *Milberry* [2003] Cr App R (S) 31.

five

1 s.3 Criminal Law (Sexual Offences) Act 2017.

2 The precursor to this offence was called 'defilement of girl under fifteen years of age' or 'unlawful carnal knowledge' and was contained in the Criminal Law Amendment Act 1935. Although the new and old offence contain definitional differences, the maximum penalty of life imprisonment remains the same. Doyle, D.M. (2024) 'Unlawful Carnal Knowledge in the Irish Free State, 1924–1935', *The Historical Journal*, 1–29.

3 *Irish Times*, 'Man gets 15 years for raping and beating daughter' (Dublin, 3 November 2018). *DPP v X* [2021] IECA 168.

4 *Mayo News*, 'Man sentenced to 15 years in 'depraved' daughter-rape case' (Dublin, 24 April 2018).

5 *thejournal.ie*, 'Rapist (75) who abused sister and his seven daughters over 23-year period jailed for 20 years' (Dublin, 15 June 2020).

6 *DPP v McC* [2020] IECA 351, para 25.

7 *Irish Times*, 'Man gets 21-year term for raping stepsons hundreds of times' (Dublin, 4 June 2016).

8 *Irish Times*, 'Father jailed for abuse and rape of three daughters over 18-year period' (Dublin, 19 May 2015).

9 *Irish Times*, '36-year sentence for brother who sexually abused boys for years' (Dublin, 24 November 1999).

10 *Irish Times*, 'Sex offender freed 18 months into 36-year sentence' (Dublin, 16 June 2001).

11 *Irish Times*, 'Judge jails father for 18 years for raping daughter from age of three' (Dublin, 21 July 2018); *DPP v Murphy* [2022] IECA 144.

12 *Irish Times*, 'Man jailed for 15 years for raping young girls' (Dublin, 6 December 1995).

13 *DPP v FE* [2019] IESC 85 [2020] 1 ILRM 517.

14 *DPP v FE* [2019] IESC 85 [2020] 1 ILRM 517.

15 *Irish Times*, 'Father jailed for abuse and rape of three daughters over 18-year period' (Dublin, 19 May 2015).

16 *DPP v FE* [2019] IESC 85 [2020] 1 ILRM 517.

17 *DPP v SC* [2019] IECA 168, para 8 [2020] 1 ILRM 517.

18 Stoltenborgh, M., Van Ijzendoorn, M.H., Euser, E.M. and Bakermans-Kranenburg, M.J. (2011) 'A global perspective on child sexual abuse: Meta-analysis of prevalence around the world', *Child Maltreatment*, *16*(2): 79–101.

19 *DPP v FE* [2019] IESC 85 [2020] 1 ILRM 517.

20 The term 'step-father' is broadly defined here and includes those described as being in a relationship with the mother and living in the home with the victim.

21 Richards, K. (2011) 'Misperceptions about child sex offenders', *Trends and Issues in Crime and Criminal Justice*, 429: 1–9.

22 *Irish Times*, 'Brother gets 18 years' jail for sex attacks' (Dublin, 28 November 1992). *DPP v M* [1994] 2 ILRM 541.

23 *Irish Times*, 'Judge jails "serial offender" former priest for sex attacks on boys' (Dublin, 7 December 2010).

24 Sexual violence here refers to unwanted contact sexual violence. See Central Statistics Office (2023) *Sexual Violence Survey 2022 – Main Results*. Dublin: Central Statistics Office.

25 *DPP v ET* [2016] IECA 312; *Irish Times*, 'Ex-prison officer gets 10 years for sex abuse of daughter' (Dublin, 30 July 2011).

26 *Mayo News*, 'Man sentenced to 15 years in 'depraved' daughter-rape case' (Dublin, 24 April 2018).

27 Cited in: *DPP v FE* [2019] IESC 85 [2020] 1 ILRM 517 para 21. This sentencing handbook is not publicly available.

28 *Irish Times*, 'Man sentenced to 18 years for child rape' (Dublin, 30 April 2013); *Irish Times*, 'Father gets 15 years for raping daughter' (Dublin, 6 November 2012).

29 *Irish Times*, 'Man given 15 years for multiple rapes of three children' (Dublin, 19 March 2014).

30 *DPP v FE* [2019] IESC 85 [2020] 1 ILRM 517.

31 *Irish Times*, 'Man admits 210 charges of abusing 5 daughters since 1976' (Dublin, 2 December 2000).

32 *DPP v J McD* [2021] IECA 31.

33 Brown, G. (2020) *Sentencing Rape: A Comparative Analysis*. Oxford: Bloomsbury Publishing, p 46.

34 *DPP v DD* [2024] Unreported, Court of Appeal, 30 July 2024.

35 *Irish Times*, 'Man (42) is jailed for life for raping boy' (Dublin, 12 October 2002).

36 Seto, M.C., Babchishin, K.M., Pullman, L.E. and McPhail, I.V. (2015) 'The puzzle of intrafamilial child sexual abuse: A meta-analysis comparing intrafamilial and extrafamilial offenders with child victims', *Clinical Psychology Review*, *39*: 42–57.

37 For an analysis, see Brown (2020), pp 16–27.

38 Seto et al (2015).

39 Seto et al (2015).

40 *DPP v Griffin* [2011] IECA 62.

41 *Irish Times*, 'Man who raped teenage girl jailed for 15 years' (Dublin, 6 February 2007).

42 *Irish Times*, '12-year sentence for rape and indecent assault of daughters' (Dublin, 7 February 2014).
43 *Irish Times*, '36-year sentence for brother who sexually abused boys for years' (Dublin, 24 November 1999).
44 *Irish Times*, '17 years for man who raped daughter' (Dublin, 22 March 1997).
45 *Irish Times*, 'Jailed for 15 years over daughter's rape' (Dublin, 27 March 2012).
46 Stroebel, S.S., O'Keefe, S.L., Beard, K.W., Kuo, S.Y., Swindell, S.V. and Kommor, M.J. (2012) 'Father–daughter incest: Data from an anonymous computerized survey', *Journal of Child Sexual Abuse*, *21*: 176–199.
47 *Irish Times*, 'Father who raped daughter for almost a decade gets 12 years' jail' (Dublin, 3 April 2014).
48 *Irish Times*, '17 years for man who raped daughter' (Dublin, 22 March 1997).
49 *Irish Times*, 'Waterford rape case: Boy continues to struggle after years of abuse' (Dublin, 10 October 2016).
50 *Irish Times*, 'Judge sentences Donegal man to 15 years in jail for sex abuse' (Dublin, 4 March 2014).
51 *DPP v D* [2004] IECCA 8.
52 Seto et al (2015).
53 Seto et al (2015).
54 Seto, M.C. (2008) *Pedophilia and Sexual Offending against Children: Theory, Assessment, and Intervention*. Washington DC: American Psychological Association.
55 It was not possible to identify references to mitigating factors in ten cases.
56 In one of these cases the defendant had pleaded guilty to some of the charges but not guilty to others.
57 It was not possible to identify the stage at which a guilty plea was entered in 14 cases.
58 *Irish Times*, 'Man (64) sentenced to 15 years for rape' (Dublin, 11 October 2008).
59 *Irish Times*, 'Man gets 15 years' jail for abuse of daughter' (Dublin, 27 May 2011). *DPP v PC* [2007] IECA 328.
60 *Irish Times*, 'Man gets 15 years for assaults, torture and mutilation of wife and daughter' (Dublin, 8 July 2000).
61 *Irish Times*, 'Man gets 15 years for assaults, torture and mutilation of wife and daughter' (Dublin, 8 July 2000).
62 Sentencing Council (2013) *Sexual Offence: Definitive Guideline*. London: Sentencing Council, p 11.
63 *Irish Times*, '17 years for man who raped daughter' (Dublin, 22 March 1997).
64 *DPP v RC* [2023] Unreported, Court of Appeal, 14 February 2023.

65 Ring, S., Gleeson, K. and Stevenson, K. (2022) *Child Sexual Abuse Reported by Adult Survivors: Legal Responses in England and Wales, Ireland and Australia*. London: Routledge, pp 132–133.
66 Ring, S. (2017) 'The victim of historical child sexual abuse in the Irish Courts 1999–2006', *Social & Legal Studies*, *26*(5): 562–580.
67 Ring et al (2022), p 152.
68 Ring et al (2022), p 155.
69 O'Malley, T. (2016) *Sentencing Law and Practice* (3rd ed). Dublin: Thomson Round Hall, p 667.
70 O'Malley (2016), p 665.
71 *Irish Times*, 'Judge jails "serial offender" former priest for sex attacks on boys' (Dublin, 7 December 2010).

six

1 O'Donnell, I. (2011) 'Criminology, Bureaucracy and Unfinished Business', in M. Bosworth and C. Hoyle (eds) *What Is Criminology?* Oxford: Oxford University Press, pp 488–501.
2 Healy, D. and Griffin, D. (2023) 'Unnesting the matryoshka doll: an ecological model of probation and parole decision-making in Ireland', *Journal of Contemporary Criminal Justice*, *39*(1): 75–93.
3 One case was decided in Cork Circuit Court as it dealt with convictions for indecent assault and the defendant was sentenced to 36 years imprisonment for 18 offences. The judge sentenced the defendant to serve 18 two-year sentences consecutively. *Irish Times*, '36-year sentence for brother who sexually abused boys for years' (Dublin, 24 November 1999).
4 Courts Service (2024) *Annual Report*. Dublin: Courts Service, p 108.
5 *Irish Independent*, 'Controversial judge who is not afraid to speak out' (Dublin, 11 October 2007).
6 Courts Service (2021) *Annual Report*. Dublin: Courts Service, p 21.
7 *Irish Independent*, 'Controversial judge who is not afraid to speak out' (Dublin, 11 October 2007).
8 Padfield, N., Liebling, A. and Arnold, H. (2000) *An Exploration of Decision-making at Discretionary Lifer Panels*. Home Office.
9 Tata, C. (2020) *Sentencing: A Social Process*. Cham: Palgrave Macmillan, p 59.
10 Tata (2020), p 6.
11 O'Malley, T. (2016) *Sentencing Law and Practice* (3rd ed). Dublin: Thomson Round Hall, p 804; *DPP v Sheedy* [2000] 2 IR 184, 190.
12 *DPP v Z* [2014] 2 ILRM 132.
13 *DPP v Z* [2014] 2 ILRM 132; *DPP v Ryan* [2014] 2 ILRM 98; *DPP v Fitzgibbon* [2014] 2 ILRM 116, 424.
14 *DPP v FE* [2019] IESC 85 [2020] 1 ILRM 517, para 38.

15 Gormley, J., O'Malley, T., Roberts, J., Spohn, C. and Tata, C. (2023) *Assessing Methodological Approaches to Sentencing Data and Analysis*. Dublin: Sentencing Guidelines and Information Committee.

16 Office of the Director of Public Prosecutions (2019) *Guidelines for Prosecutors* (5th ed). Dublin: Office of the Director of Public Prosecutions.

17 *DPP v O'Brien* [2018] IECA 2, para 35.

18 Tata (2020), p 21.

19 Franko, K.A. (2005) *Sentencing in the Age of Information: From Faust to Macintosh*. London: Glasshouse Press.

20 Brown, G. (2020) *Sentencing Rape: A Comparative Analysis*. Oxford: Bloomsbury Publishing, p 67; Ranyard, R., Hebenton, B. and Pease, K. (1994) 'An analysis of a guideline case as applied to the offence of rape', *The Howard Journal of Criminal Justice*, *33*(3): 203–217.

21 *Irish Times*, 'Teen rapist sentenced to 15 years penal servitude' (Dublin, 21 December 1994); *Irish Times*, 'Man gets 15 years for rape of his mother' (Dublin, 2 October 2012).

22 McLean, S. and Cunningham, G., 'A man was yesterday given five life sentences for the rape and assault of a woman, one of the harshest sentences for rape handed down in an Irish court', *Irish Independent* (Dublin, 30 January 2010).

23 *DPP v Conroy* [1989] ILRM 139, p 142.

24 *Irish Times*, 'Appeal court rejects application to reduce sentence for gang rape' (Dublin, 17 October 2006).

25 *Irish Times*, 'Child-abuser loses appeal against four life sentences' (Dublin, 22 December 2004); *DPP v D* [2004] Report No 126/03.

26 *Irish Times*, 'Man who treated cleaner as a slave and "sex object" jailed for 15 years' (Dublin, 31 October 2019).

27 *Irish Times*, 'Man (42) is jailed for life for raping boy' (Dublin, 12 October 2002).

28 *Irish Times*, 'Dundalk man gets 20 years for incest' (Dublin, 15 January 1994).

29 Maroney, T.A. (2011) Emotional Regulation and Judicial Behaviour, *California Law Review* 99(6): 1481–1552; Gunby, C. and Carline, A. (2020) 'The emotional particulars of working on rape cases: Doing dirty work, managing emotional dirt and conceptualizing "tempered indifference"', *The British Journal of Criminology*, *60*(2): 343–362; Anleu, S.R. and Mack, K. (2005) 'Magistrates' everyday work and emotional labour', *Journal of Law and Society*, *32*(4): 590–614.

30 Tata (2020), p 69.

31 Tata (2020), p 69.

32 *DPP v WD* [2007] IEHC 310 [2008] 1 IR 308.

33 O'Malley, T. (2017) 'Judgment and calculation in the selection of sentence', *Criminal Law Forum, 28*(3): 361–389.

34 The remaining cases related to an appeal against conviction or an appeal on another matter. In some cases, the defendant appealed against the conviction as well as the severity of sentence. Only appeals against conviction that were unsuccessful were included in the study.

35 O'Malley (2016), p 881.

36 *DPP v Redmond* [2001] 3 IR 390; O'Malley, T. (2006) *Sentencing Law and Practice* (2nd ed). Dublin: Thomson Round Hall, p 646.

37 O'Malley (2006), p 623.

38 *DPP v M* [1994] 2 I.L.R.M 541.

39 *DPP v M* [1994] 2 I.L.R.M 541.

40 s.2 Criminal Justice Act 1993.

41 *DPP v Murray* [2017] IECA 292; *Irish Times*, 'Appeal Court varies rapists' sentence' (Dublin, 14 February 2006).

42 *DPP v DD* [2024] Unreported, Court of Appeal, 30 July 2024; *DPP v AA* [2024] Unreported, Court of Appeal, 30 July 2024.

43 *DPP v R McC* [2005] IECA 105.

44 *DPP v M McC* [2020] IECA 351, para 25.

45 *DPP v Cassidy* [2019] IECA 249.

46 *Irish Times*, 'Rapist's term cut over judge's comments' (Dublin, 24 November 2007).

47 *DPP v Tiernan* [1987] IESC 190, para (D); *DPP v McCartan* [2010] IECA 50.

48 *Irish Times*, 'Sentence for rape reduced on appeal' (Dublin, 27 March 1990).

49 *DPP v* SC [2019] IECA 348.

50 Hannah-Moffat, K., Maurutto, P. and Turnbull, S. (2009) 'Negotiated risk: Actuarial illusions and discretion in probation', *Canadian Journal of Law and Society, 24*(3): 391–409.

51 Kemshall, H. (2001) *Risk Assessment and Management of Known Violent and Sexual Offenders: A Review of Current Issues*. London: Home Office.

52 *DPP v Tiernan* [1989] ILRM 149, 250.

53 O'Morain, P. (1996) 'Guilty plea of more benefit to the rapist than the victim Judges should be given the discretion to impose life sentences on rapists who have pleaded guilty, says the Dublin Rape Crisis Centre', *Irish Times* (10 August 1996), 8.

54 *DPP v G* [1994] 1 IR 587.

55 *Attorney General v X* [1992] IESC 1.

56 Sheridan, K. (1995) 'A good family man', *Irish Times* (18 March 1995).

57 Sheridan, K. (1995) 'A good family man', *Irish Times* (18 March 1995).

58 Brennock, M. (1995) 'Judge says prior rulings disallow life sentence on multiple child rapist', *Irish Times* (6 December 1995).

[59] Brennock, M. (1995) 'Judge says prior rulings disallow life sentence on multiple child rapist', *Irish Times* (6 December 1995).
[60] Brennock, M. (1995) 'Owen to study court remarks on life sentences', *Irish Times* (6 December 1995).
[61] s.29.
[62] *DPP v McC and CD* [2007] IESC 47 [2008] 1 ILRM 321.
[63] *DPP v Conroy* [1988] IESC 66 [1989] ILRM 139 [142].
[64] Tata (2020), p 2.
[65] Kilcommins, S., O'Donnell, I., O'Sullivan, E. and Vaughan, B. (2004) *Crime, Punishment and the Search for Order in Ireland*. Dublin: Institute of Public Administration, p 193.
[66] Kilcommins et al (2004); Griffin, D. and O'Donnell, I. (2012) 'The life sentence and parole', *The British Journal of Criminology*, *52*(3): 611–629.
[67] s.5 Criminal Justice Act 1993 as amended by the Criminal Procedure Act 2010.
[68] *DPP v C(W)* [1994] 1 ILRM 321.
[69] s.10 Bail Act 1997.
[70] *DPP v Cummins* [2008] IECA 92.

seven

[1] Tata, C. (2020) *Sentencing: A Social Process*. Cham: Palgrave Macmillan, p 60.
[2] Tata (2020), p 51.
[3] O'Malley, T. (2017) 'Judgment and calculation in the selection of sentence', *Criminal Law Forum*, *28*(3): 361–389.
[4] *Delaney v The Personal Injuries Assessment Board, the Judicial Council and the Attorney General* [2014] IESC 10.

References

Aas, K.F. (2012) '"The earth is one but the world is not": Criminological theory and its geopolitical divisions', *Theoretical Criminology*, *16*(1): 5–20.

Aebi, M.F., Cocco, E. and Molnar, L. (2023) *SPACE I–Annual Penal Statistics: Prison Populations 2022*. Strasbourg: Council of Europe and University of Lausanne.

Anleu, S.R. and Mack, K. (2005) 'Magistrates' everyday work and emotional labour', *Journal of Law and Society*, *32*(4): 590–614.

Ashworth, A. and Padfield, N. (2015) 'Editorial – Five years of the Sentencing Council', *Criminal Law Review*: 657–658.

Ashworth, A. and Wasik, M. (2018) 'Sentencing the multiple offender', in J. Ryberg, J.V. Roberts and J.W. De Keijser (eds) *Sentencing Multiple Crimes*. Oxford: Oxford University Press, p 211.

Borum, R., Swartz, M. and Swanson, J. (1996) 'Assessing and managing violence risk in clinical practice', *Journal of Psychiatric Practice*, *2*(4): 205–215.

Brown, G. (2017) *Criminal Sentencing as Practical Wisdom*. Oxford: Hart Publishing.

Brown, G. (2020) *Sentencing Rape: A Comparative Analysis*. Oxford: Bloomsbury Publishing.

Cassell, P.G. (2008) 'In defense of victim impact statements', *Ohio State Journal of Criminal Law*, *6*: 611.

Central Statistics Office (2022) *Recorded Crime Detention 2021*. Dublin: Central Statistics Office.

Central Statistics Office (2023) *Sexual Violence Survey 2022 – Main Results*. Dublin: Central Statistics Office.

Central Statistics Office (2024) *Recorded Crime Detention 2023*. Dublin: Central Statistics Office.

Christie, N. (1986) 'The ideal victim', in E.A. Fattah (ed) *From Crime Policy to Victim Policy: Reorienting the Justice System*. London: Palgrave Macmillan UK, pp 17–30.

Courts Service (2021–24) *Annual Reports*. Dublin: Courts Service.

Conroy, B. and Gunning, P. (2009) 'The Irish sentencing information system (ISIS): A practical guide to a practical tool', *Judicial Studies Institute Journal, 1*, 37–53.

Corr, M., O'Mahony, P., Lovett, J. and Kelly, L. (2009) *Different Systems, Similar Outcomes? Tracking Attrition in Reported Rape Cases in Eleven Countries (Country Briefing: Ireland)*. London: Child and Woman Abuse Studies Unit.

Department of Justice, Equality and Law Reform (2009) *The Management of Sex Offenders: A Discussion Document*. Dublin: Department of Justice and Law Reform.

Doyle, D.M. (2012) 'Reasonable belief and unlawful carnal knowledge: A historical perspective', *Irish Jurist, 47*, 49–75.

Doyle, D.M. (2024) 'Unlawful carnal knowledge in the Irish Free State, 1924–1935', *The Historical Journal*, 1–29, doi:10.1017/S0018246X24000190.

Ellison, L. and Munro, V.E. (2010) 'A stranger in the bushes, or an elephant in the room? Critical reflections upon received rape myth wisdom in the context of a mock jury study', *New Criminal Law Review, 13*(4): 781–801.

Engen, R.L. and Gainey, R.R. (2000) 'Modeling the effects of legally relevant and extralegal factors under sentencing guidelines: The rules have changed', *Criminology, 38*(4): 1207–1230.

Estrich, S. (1987) *Real Rape: How the Legal System Victimizes Women Who Say No*. Cambridge, MA: Harvard University Press.

Franko, K.A. (2005) *Sentencing in the Age of Information: From Faust to Macintosh*. London: Glasshouse Press.

Freiberg, A. and Roberts, J.V. (2023) 'March. Sentencing commissions and guidelines: A case study in policy transfer', *Criminal Law Forum, 34*(1): 87–129.

Ghandnoosh, N. (2017) *Delaying a Second Chance: The Declining Prospects for Parole on Life Sentences*. Washington DC: Sentencing Project.

Gormley, J., O'Malley, T., Roberts, J., Spohn, C. and Tata, C. (2023) *Assessing Methodological Approaches to Sentencing Data and Analysis*. Dublin: Sentencing Guidelines and Information Committee.

Griffin, D. (2018) *Killing Time: Life Imprisonment and Parole in Ireland*. Cham: Palgrave Macmillan.

Griffin, D. (2020) 'Life imprisonment and the Parole Act 2019: Assessing the potential impact on parole decision-making', *Irish Judicial Studies Journal 4*(1): 24–44.

Griffin, D. (2015) 'The release and recall of life sentence prisoners: Policy, practice and politics', *Irish Jurist, 53*: 1–35.

Griffin, D. (2024) ' "Dangerous" and "Devious": Exploring judicial rationales when imposing a discretionary sentence of life imprisonment', *Irish Judicial Studies Journal, 8*(1): 1–18.

Griffin, D. and Healy, D. (2019) 'The pains of parole for life sentence prisoners in Ireland: Risk, rehabilitation and re-entry', *European Journal of Probation, 11*(3): 124–138.

Griffin, D. and O'Donnell, I. (2012) 'The life sentence and parole', *The British Journal of Criminology, 52*(3): 611–629.

Griffin, D. and O'Donnell, I. (2016) 'Confusingly compliant with the European Convention on Human Rights: The release of life sentence prisoners in Ireland', in D. Van Zyl Smit and C. Appleton (eds) *Life Imprisonment and Human Rights*. Oxford: Hart Publishing, pp 267–288.

Guiry, R. (2006) 'Who is the victim? The use of victim impact statements in murder and manslaughter cases', *Irish Criminal Law Journal, 6*(3): 2.

Gunby, C. and Carline, A. (2020) 'The emotional particulars of working on rape cases: Doing dirty work, managing emotional dirt and conceptualizing "tempered indifference"', *The British Journal of Criminology, 60*(2): 343–362.

Hannah-Moffat, K., Maurutto, P. and Turnbull, S. (2009) 'Negotiated risk: Actuarial illusions and discretion in probation', *Canadian Journal of Law and Society, 24*(3): 391–409.

Hanly, C., Healy, D. and Scriver, S. (2009) *Rape & Justice in Ireland: A National Study of Survivor, Prosecutor and Court Responses to Rape*. Dublin: The Liffey Press.

Healy, D. and O'Donnell, I. (2010) 'Crime, consequences and court reports', *Irish Criminal Law Journal, 20*(1): 2–7.

Healy, D. and Griffin, D. (2023) 'Unnesting the matryoshka doll: An ecological model of probation and parole decision-making in Ireland', *Journal of Contemporary Criminal Justice, 39*(1): 75–93.

Hogan, G. and Whyte, G. (2004) *The Irish Constitution* (4th ed). Dublin: Butterworths.

Howard League for Penal Reform (2024) *Sentencing Inflation: A Judicial Critique*, London: Howard League for Penal Reform.

Jewkes, M. (2004) 'Media representations of the causes of crime', *Criminal Justice Matters, 55*(1): 26–27.

Joint Committee on Justice, Defence and Equality (2013) *Report on Penal Reform*. Dublin: Stationery Office.

Jones, J.S., Wynn, B.N., Kroeze, B., Dunnuck, C. and Rossman, L. (2004) 'Comparison of sexual assaults by strangers versus known assailants in a community-based population', *The American Journal of Emergency Medicine, 22*(6): 454–459.

Kemshall, H. (2001) *Risk Assessment and Management of Known Violent and Sexual Offenders: A Review of Current Issues*. London: Home Office.

Kilcommins, S., O'Donnell, I., O'Sullivan, E. and Vaughan, B. (2004) *Crime, Punishment and the Search for Order in Ireland*. Dublin: Institute of Public Administration.

Leahy, S. (2014) 'Bad laws or bad attitudes? Assessing the impact of societal attitudes upon the conviction rate for rape in Ireland', *Irish Journal of Applied Social Studies, 14*(1): 18–29.

Maguire, N. and Carr, N. (2017) *Probation Service Research Report: Individualising Justice: Pre-sentence Reports in the Irish Criminal Justice System*. Dublin: The Probation Service.

Maroney, T.A. (2011) 'Emotional regulation and judicial behaviour', *California Law Review, 99*(6): 1481–1552.

McCall-Hosenfeld, J.S., Freund, K.M. and Liebschutz, J.M. (2009) 'Factors associated with sexual assault and time to presentation', *Preventive Medicine*, *48*(6): 593–595.

McLean, S. and Cunningham, G. (2010) 'A man was yesterday given five life sentences for the rape and assault of a woman, one of the harshest sentences for rape handed down in an Irish court', *Irish Independent* (Dublin, 30 January 2010).

McGee H., Garavan R., de Barra M., Byrne J. and Conroy R. (2002) *The SAVI Report: Sexual Abuse and Victimization in Ireland*. Dublin: The Liffey Press.

Ministry of Justice, Home Office and the Office for National Statistics (2013) *An Overview of Sexual Offending in England and Wales – Statistics Bulletin*. London, Ministry of Justice, Home Office and the Office for National Statistics.

Möller, A.S., Bäckström, T., Söndergaard, H.P. and Helström, L. (2012) 'Patterns of injury and reported violence depending on relationship to assailant in female Swedish sexual assault victims', *Journal of Interpersonal Violence*, *27*(16): 3131–3148.

O'Cathaoir, K. (2012) *Recent Rape Sentencing Analysis: The WD Case & Beyond*. Dublin: Judicial Researchers Office. [No longer publicly available.]

O'Connell, M. (1999) 'Is Irish public opinion towards crime distorted by media bias?', *European Journal of Communication*, *14*(2): 191–212.

O'Donnell, I. (2011) 'Criminology, bureaucracy and unfinished business', in M. Bosworth and C. Hoyle (eds) *What Is Criminology?* Oxford: Oxford University Press.

Office of the Director of Public Prosecutions (2019) *Guidelines for Prosecutors* (5th ed). Dublin: Office of the Director of Public Prosecutions.

O'Malley, T. (2001) 'Principled discretion: Towards the development of a sentencing canon', *The Bar Review*, 7(3): 135–139.

O'Malley, T. (2003) 'Sentencing values and sentencing structures', *Judicial Studies Institute Journal*, *3*(1): 130–147.

O'Malley, T. (2009) *The Criminal Process*. Dublin: Thomas Reuters.

O'Malley, T. (2011) *Sentencing: Towards a Coherent System*. Dublin: Round Hall.

O'Malley, T. (2013) *Sexual Offences* (2nd ed). Dublin: Round Hall.

O'Malley, T. (2014) 'A quiet revolution occurred this month: Sentencing guidelines were introduced: Consistency in sentencing is sensible, provided there is flexibility to cater for exceptional cases', *Irish Times* (Dublin, 31 March 2014).

O'Malley, T. (2016) *Sentencing Law and Practice* (3rd ed). Dublin: Thomson Round Hall.

O'Malley, T. (2017) 'Judgment and calculation in the selection of sentence', *Criminal Law Forum*, *28*(3): 361–389.

O'Malley, T. (2023) 'Annual distinguished lecture 2023: From practical wisdom to guidelines: The future of sentencing regulation', Galway: University of Galway (11 May 2023).

O'Toole, M. (2024) *Report of the Scoping Inquiry into Historical Sexual Abuse in Day and Boarding Schools Run by Religious Orders*. Dublin: Education Scoping Inquiry.

Padfield, N. and Roberts, J.V. (2011) 'Intoxication as a sentencing factor: Mitigation or aggravation', in J.V. Roberts (ed) *Mitigation and Aggravating at Sentencing*. Cambridge: Cambridge University Press, pp 81–101.

Padfield, N., Liebling, A. and Arnold, H. (2000) *An Exploration of Decision-Making at Discretionary Lifer Panels*. London: Home Office.

Pina-Sánchez, J. and Linacre, R. (2013) 'Sentence consistency in England and Wales: Evidence from the Crown Court sentencing survey', *British Journal of Criminology*, *53*(6): 1118–1138.

Pina-Sánchez, J., Gosling, J.P., Chung, H.I., Bourgeois, E., Geneletti, S. and Marder, I.D. (2019) 'Have the England and Wales guidelines affected sentencing severity? An empirical analysis using a scale of severity and time-series analyses', *British Journal of Criminology*, *59*(4): 979–1001.

Prison Service (2012–2024) *Annual Reports*. Dublin and Longford: Irish Prison Service.

Ranyard, R., Hebenton, B.I.L.L, and Pease, K. (1994) 'An analysis of a guideline case as applied to the offence of rape', *The Howard Journal of Criminal Justice*, *33*(3): 203–217.

Richards, K. (2011) 'Misperceptions about child sex offenders', *Trends and Issues in Crime and Criminal Justice*, *429*: 1–9.

Ring, S. (2017) 'The victim of historical child sexual abuse in the Irish Courts 1999–2006', *Social & Legal Studies*, *26*(5): 562–580.

Ring, S., Gleeson, K. and Stevenson, K. (2022) *Child Sexual Abuse Reported by Adult Survivors: Legal Responses in England and Wales, Ireland and Australia*. London: Routledge.

Roberts, J.V. (1997) 'The role of criminal record in the sentencing process', *Crime and Justice*, *22*: 303–362.

Roberts, J.V. (2019) 'The evolution of sentencing guidelines in Minnesota and England and Wales', *Crime and Justice*, *48*(1): 187–253.

Roberts, J.V. and Erez, E. (2004) 'Communication in sentencing: Exploring the expressive function of victim impact statements', *International Review of Victimology*, *10*(3): 223–244.

Rubin, A.T. and Phelps, M.S. (2017) 'Fracturing the penal state: State actors and the role of conflict in penal change', *Theoretical Criminology*, *21*(4): 422–440.

Ryberg, J., Roberts, J.V. and De Keijser, J.W. (eds) (2018) *Sentencing Multiple Crimes*. Oxford: Oxford University Press.

Sentencing Council of England and Wales (2013) *Sexual Offences Definitive Guideline*. London: Sentencing Council of England and Wales.

Sentencing Guidelines Council (2007) *Sexual Offences Act 2003 – Definitive Guidelines*. London: Sentencing Guidelines Council.

Seto, M.C. (2008) *Pedophilia and Sexual Offending against Children: Theory, Assessment, and Intervention*. Washington DC: American Psychological Association.

Seto, M.C., Babchishin, K.M., Pullman, L.E. and McPhail, I.V. (2015) 'The puzzle of intrafamilial child sexual abuse: A meta-analysis comparing intrafamilial and extrafamilial offenders with child victims', *Clinical Psychology Review*, *39*: 42–57.

Sheleff, L. (1987) *Ultimate Penalties: Capital Punishment, Life Imprisonment, Physical Torture*. Columbus: Ohio State University Press.

Sheridan, K. (1995) 'A good family man', *Irish Times* (18 March 1995).

Steffensmeier, D., Ulmer, J. and Kramer, J. (1998) 'The interaction of race, gender, and age in criminal sentencing: The punishment cost of being young, black, and male', *Criminology*, *36*(4): 763–798.

Stermac, L., Bove, G.D. and Addison, M. (2001) 'Violence, injury, and presentation patterns in spousal sexual assaults', *Violence Against Women*, 7(11): 1218–1233.

Stith, K. and Cabranes, J. (1998) *Fear of Judging: Sentencing Guidelines in the Federal Courts*. Chicago: Chicago University Press.

Stoltenborgh, M., Van Ijzendoorn, M.H., Euser, E.M. and Bakermans-Kranenburg, M.J. (2011) 'A global perspective on child sexual abuse: Meta-analysis of prevalence around the world', *Child Maltreatment*, *16*(2): 79–101.

Stroebel, S.S., O'Keefe, S.L., Beard, K.W., Kuo, S.Y., Swindell, S.V. and Kommor, M.J. (2012) 'Father–daughter incest: Data from an anonymous computerized survey', *Journal of Child Sexual Abuse*, *21*: 176–199.

Tata, C. (2007) 'Sentencing as craftwork and the binary epistemologies of the discretionary decision process', *Social & Legal Studies*, *16*(3): 425–447.

Tata, C. (2020) *Sentencing: A Social Process*. Cham: Palgrave Macmillan.

Temkin, J. and Krahé, B. (2008) *Sexual Assault and the Justice Gap: A Question of Attitude* (1st ed). Oxford: Hart.

Tonry, M. (1996) *Sentencing Matters*. New York: Oxford University Press.

Tonry, M. (2007) 'Determinants of penal policies', *Crime and Justice*, *36*(1): 1–48.

United Nations Centre for Social Development and Humanitarian Affairs Crime Prevention and Criminal Justice Branch (1994) *Life Imprisonment*. Vienna: United Nations.

van Zyl Smit, D. and Appleton, C. (2019) *Life Imprisonment: A Global Human Rights Analysis*. Harvard: Harvard University Press.

Wasik, M. (2003) 'Sentencing guidelines: Past, present, and future', *Current Legal Problems*, *56*(1): 239–264.

Wieberneit, M., Thal, S., Clare, J., Notebaert, L. and Tubex, H. (2024) 'Silenced survivors: A systematic review of the barriers to reporting, investigating, prosecuting, and sentencing of adult female rape and sexual assault', *Trauma, Violence, & Abuse*, *25*(5): 3742–3757.

Index

Page numbers in **bold** type refer to tables.

R

S

T

U

V

W

X

Y